Language, Reading and Learning

LANGUAGE, READING AND LEARNING

edited by

Asher Cashdan

UNIVERSITY PARK PRESS *Baltimore*

First published in the United States 1979 by
University Park Press,
233 East Redwood Street,
Baltimore, Maryland 21202

**Library of Congress Cataloging in
Publication data**

Main entry under title:

Language, reading, and learning.
1. Language arts—Addresses, essays,
   lectures.
I. Cashdan, Asher.
LB1575.8.L37   420'.7   78-24590
ISBN 0-8391-1365-X

Printed in Great Britain
by Billing and Sons Ltd.
London, Guildford and Worcester.

Contents

Introduction

Throughout the world concern about the learning and teaching of language skills has been growing apace among parents, teachers and governments in the past decade. Educators in particular have slowly come to acknowledge that its four aspects – listening, talking, reading and writing – need to be integrated in the learner's development and that they cannot be taught in piecemeal fashion. It has been realized also that many of the responsibilities in this field which had till recently been largely pushed on to the shoulders of English or remedial specialists must now be shared around the school, not merely as a matter of fairness but for some other very positive reasons. Science teachers, mathematicians, modern linguists and all the rest need to plan a co-ordinated policy for spoken and written language. School could then become an organic whole for the pupil – in the secondary school especially such a reorganization has been long overdue.

In 1975 these concerns were crystallized in Britain by the publication of the British government enquiry into language and reading, the Bullock Report (DES, 1975). This gave authoritative support to the development of school language policies and to planned developmental language teaching for all pupils. It paid particular attention to the links between different stages in schooling and to the working-out of 'language across the curriculum' schemes, particularly in secondary schools.

   The later seventies are showing the effects of such thinking and recommendations, in Britain and elsewhere. The keen and the committed have made progress. Local initiatives have been taken in a variety of contexts and here and there exciting work is going on. But there are still large numbers of schools quite untouched by recent educational thinking as well as many who pay little more than lip-service to what it implies in practical teaching and in the organization of the curriculum.

   In producing this book, we hope to reach both those who are already actively involved in new teaching approaches and, if we are lucky, some of those who have not yet joined in. What was advocated in the early 1970s is now, we think, not enough. Life moves on, even in the classroom. We not only have fresh ideas, but more experience of how to work them out in practice and more appreciation of what precisely is needed. It is no longer simply a question of trying to put existing ideas into practice; the argument needs to be carried several stages further.

   We have chosen in this book to focus on 'mainstream' issues. So there are no chapters on immigrants, remedial teaching, adult literacy or other such topics. This is not because we consider them unimportant, but because a deeper perception of what goes on, and what the needs are in the 'normal' classroom should illuminate these areas also. One possible exception is the chapter by Alan Davies on lessons from second language teaching. But what Davies has to say is of relevance to the whole of language work in schools, so that what he provides can be seen as a comparative perspective on our main task, rather than as an expression of sectional interest. Again, whether our readers are more concerned with primary or with secondary education, they should find all the chapters relevant to their interests. For the issues dealt with and, in our view, the method of their treatment, are not narrowly confined to any one age-group or setting.

   The chapters in this book are written by a variety of contributors with differing backgrounds and specialities. But it seems reasonable to suggest that there is a single message running through all their contributions. This is that the job of the teacher in the 1980s demands an application and a degree of technical expertise considerably in advance of what has been required in the past. The so-called 'progressive' movement in education has been much maligned: it has often been hinted, or even claimed openly, that the progressive teacher stands aside and watches the child teaching himself. This claim embodies both an important truth and a foolish lie. The truth lies in the fact that the teacher has to move away from the role of classroom tyrant and controller, to a mode of interaction that allows pupils to make their own understandings, to achieve their own learning. The lie is the suggestion that this reduces the amount of work the teacher has to do. In fact, the teacher who operates effectively in an 'open' structure has much more to do; such a teacher has to plan, to record, to diagnose, to know when to stand back and when to provide learning frameworks. David Crystal and Denis Vincent in their chapters make clear how much the teacher needs to know to be able to diagnose, advise and assess effectively. The subtleties of language development, of learning to read and of learning from one's reading, are developed in the chapters by Alan Davies, Eric Lunzer and Terry Dolan and by Geoffrey Roberts. And it is in the writing of Bernard Harrison, of Elizabeth and David Grugeon, and of Mike Torbe that the difficult balance between intervention and restraint, where the child is groping after meanings, is really highlighted for the perceptive teacher.

The goals we set in education are both affective and cognitive. We want to see our pupils developing socially, emotionally and intellectually; indeed these are but different facets of human personality which we separate for analysis, but which in the real person cannot and should not be separated. Nevertheless, as teachers we are not always successful in integrating our affective and cognitive goals, whether in our educational thinking or our practice; in the Bullock Report, for instance, it was quite clear that the sections on literature came from different stables from those on reading skills. In this volume, too, a full integration is not yet achieved, although we are moving in the right direction. It is noticeable in how many chapters in the book contributors are concerned to stress that neither skills without meanings, nor meanings without technical competence, will do on their own. But we must remember also that in *speaking, listening, reading* and *writing* different skills, techniques and understandings are inevitably involved. The spoken and the written languages are not mirror images of one another; they differ significantly both in nature and in function. What we hope to give our students is more than just a feeling for the unity of all their learning; rather, a realistic insight into its diversity.

Asher Cashdan
July 1978

Reference

Department of Education and Science (1975) *A Language for Life* (The Bullock Report). London. HMSO.

1

Language at Home and in the Classroom

ASHER CASHDAN

Reading the works of educationalists and talking to teachers one often gets the feeling that there are two school worlds. In one, pupils are eager to learn; they know what school is about, what facilities it has to offer and how to take best advantage of them. In the other, children are ill-prepared, apathetic, uninterested or even hostile. They see little purpose in studying. When they do work it is to please the teacher rather than to gain something for themselves. Teachers in this world have to work very hard, putting in the 'missing' background, getting the children interested, helping them to adjust to what is perceived as a difficult situation for them, all before learning can take place. Perhaps, rather, there are two types of children, learners and non-learners. It would amount to much the same thing.

This chapter attempts to find out how much this picture is a caricature and how much it reflects reality. It is necessary to ask questions about children and their development, what happens to them in the first few years of life and how the schools treat them, not just when they arrive, but right through their educational careers.

1

Homes and parents

Let us begin in the home. It has long been considered obvious that families vary in the contributions they make to their children's educability. The correlation between social class and achievement in school has been documented over and over. Burt (1937) drew attention to this in his early work. The issue was pursued by the researches of Wiseman and Warburton (see Wiseman, 1964) and further demonstrated in subsequent longitudinal studies (beginning with Douglas, 1964).

However, correlational research tells us little about what is actually happening: the correlation which Wiseman found between the number of books in the home and school attainment (Plowden, DES 1967) leads us to suggest that if books are there, their use (or perhaps some associated behaviour) is conducive to school attainment. But such measures tell us nothing of relevant behaviours. In the same way, socio-economic status may be an indication of other things that matter — in itself it means nothing. What we need is a measure of relevant *behaviour*. It is for this reason that researchers such as Hess and Shipman (1965) have been much quoted. They recorded parents talking to their children, helping them to solve problems and demonstrating their teaching styles. Some of the differences they found have been dismissed as due to the rather artificial (laboratory-style) situation in which the data were collected; nevertheless, this seems the kind of research that is needed.

Bernstein's research in the 1960s (see Bernstein, 1971) was exciting because it was about process — the postulated, elaborated and restricted codes. It took some time for it to become clear that linguistically the codes could hardly be justified. Many still think that Bernstein put his finger on something important: that certain types of families (distinguished perhaps more for the level of education of the parents than by their social class membership) probably used speech differently, and consistently so. Some parents encourage their children to express their thoughts in words, to argue, to see themselves as differentiated persons with their own ideas and (intellectual) rights. In other settings, language may be less used, or certainly the dominant mode may be in terms of status and position rather than of personal differentiation. Admittedly, we would now want to make a number of qualifications: Rosen has pointed out that the world cannot be divided into working-class and middle-class in two neat camps; Labov (1969) has produced actual data to show that in some 'disadvantaged' cultures verbosity is common and possibly conceptual thinking is as well. Finally Swift (1966) in an interesting discussion of 'mobility-pessimism' shows how family attitudes that encourage school success cannot be neatly assigned to the middle- as opposed to the working-class.

What all this amounts to is that we should probably not be looking for large groups in society whose language is poor or non-existent, or who speak in inferior codes. We may indeed find some whose dialect is different, but that will have nothing to do with their intellectual capability (Trudgill, 1975). Many such children will, however, be likely to find school a strange place, will not fall quickly into line with its language demands and will need help in seeing both how and *why* they should talk in certain ways. At the heart of this question is the relationship between the parent and the school. In our two hypothetical situations above, the main distinguishing feature will be that some parents both understand and share the school's aims for their children, while others do not.

The case is not, however, made stronger by bringing in the linguistic nativists. Chomsky's espousal of the McNeill L.A.D. (Language Acquisition Device) should not be seen as a claim that children teach themselves language and that the parent is thus somehow redundant. Without hearing language no one is likely to develop it in one generation. The important issue, however, lies in what the minimum requirements are. Probably we used to put them too high; in fact, children will probably develop good language with relatively small exposure to good models — but they certainly do need enough, even if we suspect that enough is not all that much. The same probably applies to the Bernstein 'codes'. Children from 'restricted' backgrounds would be unlikely to use language in an elaborated way if they had never heard it so used; but a relatively low exposure probably suffices.

Furthermore, one could quote a whole range of recent developmental research that shows how wrong we have been to think of even the small child as someone we have to teach, rather than as an active learner. Trevarthen (1974) has not only demonstrated the 'conversational' capacity of infants a few weeks old; he has shown them taking the lead in early conversational interaction. Much later, the whole thrust of Goodman's (1967) work is to show that the child does not approach the text to be read as a series of marks on the page to be translated first into sounds and then into meaningful communication, but that he does all three at the same time. His search for meaning is there from the very beginning; if it dies, this may be our fault.

The Bullock Report (DES, 1975) lists a number of language uses from the work of Joan Tough, which in the committee's view

> children from 'educating' homes seem to have developed more extensively than children without these home advantages.

These language uses include:

> collaborating towards agreed ends;
>
> projecting into the future, anticipating and predicting;
>
> projecting and comparing possible alternatives,

and so on.

Note, however, the careful qualification; one group has 'developed more extensively'; yet *both* groups have the relevant language functions. Later in the same paragraph, the report talks of the more advantaged child as 'more likely to be led to use language of a higher order. . . .' In other words, both groups of children probably have this capability; the question is how much it is exercised *in the relevant school situation*.

Educational goals

At this point, it seems important to emphasize how easy it is to take for granted our educational aims, their natural authority and their associated power to command general assent. The teacher knows what the 'desired product characteristics' are. The teacher wants to make all his or her pupils literate and numerate. He has a set of goals for their academic attainment and for character and moral development as well. And while there is a range of opinion among teachers as to what they are striving for, it is quite unusual, and in the case of young children, unheard of, for the client to be consulted. Despite the fact that fewer than a hundred years have passed since, even in our advanced society we even began to make education universal and compulsory, we now take it for granted that everyone both wants to become, and can become, reasonably literate. In the earlier part of the century, failure in school was often attributed to lack of ability, probably innately determined. Today, we are less likely to hide behind that argument; we agree that literacy is within the grasp of all but the most severely handicapped. It follows, then, that some people must actually not wish to be literate. We then take it for granted that a judicious use of the stick and the carrot will do the trick. We rarely stop to question our rights (or perhaps obligations) as educators of imposing our view of education on those in our charge.

My purpose in raising these questions at this point is to pave the way for two further sections in this chapter. In the next one, we shall examine some of what is taken for granted in the classroom situation. Following that, there are questions to be asked about the child's wishes and needs.

The teacher in the classroom

I have just been suggesting that teachers are not always as aware as they might be of what is taken for granted in the situation in which they operate. We can certainly add that teachers, like other groups in work situations, are typically unaware of their own behaviour. Bullock summarized the evidence on the amount of teacher talk in the classroom. Teachers talk much more of the time than they realize; pupils do very little 'talking to learn'; for that matter they do relatively little reading to learn, as Lunzer and his colleagues have shown in their research (see, for instance, Chapter 5 in this volume). Furthermore, the balance of classroom events is very uneven. Garner (1973) demonstrated how certain types of children are addressed much more often than others; he contrasts docile girls with active boys; and little acumen is needed to guess what type of teacher verbalization the latter group attracts! In our own pilot study, Janet Philps and I (1975) found that teachers sometimes talked more to pupils whom they considered to be functioning well, even when they thought of themselves as working especially hard with children who were in particular need. It seems likely that we shall be getting similar findings in our main study.

Most people would now agree that the 'classic' study of Rosenthal and Jacobson (1968) did not really establish that mere teacher expectation that pupils would do well or badly would actually produce such a result — the research design was inadequate to sustain such a conclusion. Nevertheless, more careful documentation of a variety of studies, as in Pidgeon (1970), certainly does suggest that what the teacher expects of a pupil exerts a tremendous influence on his eventual attainment. Furthermore, teachers make up their minds about what to expect of a child on the basis of a variety of evidence, some of it misleading and secondhand (see, for example, Goodacre's study, 1968). Clearly, then, it would be dangerous to start by considering any child as 'defective' — as coming from an inadequate background. Beginning like that merely makes it likely that the child will confirm one's expectations. In any case, as I have already suggested in considering the home situation, it seems much more meaningful to think in terms of a competence-performance distinction. In other words, as Cazden (1970) pointed out some time ago, there is plenty of evidence that children of a wide variety of backgrounds do acquire language structures without difficulty. The problem is how well will they make use of them. Again, as I have already suggested, we must be very careful not to confuse language form with language function. Many children may not speak in the 'correct' classroom accent, dialect or vocabulary. But their competence in language may be as good as, or often better than, that of those who speak more acceptably. This area is well discussed in Trudgill (1975) and in Edwards (1976).

However, as both Alan Davies and Geoffrey Roberts point out elsewhere in this volume, it would be simple-minded to claim that all we have to do is to accept the child's language as a means of showing him that he is acceptable. For one thing, the standard language often has advantages for educational purposes. Some might challenge this claim; but they can hardly question the point when it comes to reading. For reading is *never* speaking. The argument that reading material provided for children should be *nearer* to 'oral speech written down' is a fair one. Too much classroom material is entirely artificial, corresponding neither to oral language nor to any written material outside its own genre. The answer, however, is not to get closer to the child's speech, but to help him to see why written language is not the same as his own speech—a point that applies to the standard speaker as well as to the 'non-standard' one.

There is one further cautionary note to be sounded. Most teachers intuitively — or because of what they have been told and what they have read — assume that they are competent to decide exactly what, and in what order, the child shall learn. So they feed the child with carefully graded material; they teach letters singly and then in combination; they start with Look and Say and follow this with phonics and so on. But it might often behoove us to be more modest. Of course, teaching is a prescriptive activity; Roberts is just one of the contributors in this volume who offer a very carefully worked-out set of prescriptions. On the other hand, flexibility in teaching means being alert to the child's learning style, being prepared to offer information as it is wanted rather than feeding it out — often, quite simply, to tell the child when he does not know. This might mean, for instance, allowing the child to go right through a book, even if he is not yet able to 'read' every word in it and for him then to pass on to another one if that is the right style for the particular child. What the teacher should often be doing — and with no loss of professional dignity — is monitoring learning rather than controlling it.

Motivation and the match

All normal children want to learn. This is obvious to anyone who studies babies and small infants. The small child has an insatiable hunger to learn and he practises continually the skills he is currently adding to his repertoire. He learns motor skills, language and conceptual thinking and social skills. He seems to need no urging. Piaget, who has spent more than fifty years studying the intellectual development of the child, has hardly felt it necessary to devote any substantial attention to motivation. He sees motivation as inherent in the developmental task. Children are intrinsically motivated.

They want to learn what is next for them to learn. Hunt (1969) has elaborated on this view. Left to himself, the small child picks the right learning diet (as he would with food). He is 'turned on' by the right-sized gap between where he is now and where he could next be. If a particular skill has been thoroughly acquired and practised it loses its motivating quality. On the other hand, a new skill which demands too much is too frustrating a challenge. The child is always on the alert to select what is difficult enough to be a challenge, but easy enough for him to achieve.

When the teacher takes over, he has to be careful to maintain this match. This is the key to successful teaching. Where demands are too low, the child will become bored and uninterested, even frustrated. On the other hand, demands that cannot be satisfied leave the child equally frustrated and fed up. The danger in classroom (as in all) learning is that 'matching' may be set aside in favour of extrinsic motivation, in favour of persuading the learner to engage in the task for some reward outside it. This may take the form of teacher praise, token rewards, and in appropriate circumstances, money or food.

People certainly will work for extrinsic rewards — if this were not so, many jobs in our society would be quite unfillable. In industry, work that is boring, dull or difficult contributes to absenteeism, employee unrest, low productivity and so on; this is also true in the classroom. If we add to a poor match between task and learner, a classroom situation where the extrinsic rewards are not working well — where teacher praise, for instance, is either not forthcoming or not valued — then it is surprising that many children learn anything in school at all.

Furthermore, it is often difficult to spot the malaise at the beginning. For at first, many children are at least willing to give the system a try. They work away at boring readers and meaningless sums to please the teacher, or perhaps in the hope of getting something out of it in the end. When both of these motivations begin to fail — the teacher ceases to be rewarding and the task fails to become meaningful — it is often too late to restore the situation. The child adjusts to being a non-learner and often it will be too late to regain lost time.

It is in the light of this analysis that we can see the strengths of the good parent and the good teacher. As White (1973) and his colleagues have demonstrated, the best parents seem to be those who do not ape the stereotypic teacher, but those who act as 'consultants' to their children. Such parents are available to answer questions, to make suggestions, to give the occasional nudge or direction. They leave the child in charge of his own learning and hence the match is likely to be of the right magnitude. The nursery teacher behaves in a similar fashion to the good parent. However, unlike the child's mother, the teacher is actually *expected* to teach the child things — and this expectation puts pressure on the teacher to make difficult decisions as to aims and balance.

Good teaching

Nothing I have said in this chapter is meant to take away from the need for the teacher to teach. The nursery teacher, though much admired, particularly outside Great Britain, is in fact in danger of abdicating too much. He or she is trained to work so hard at providing an environment in which learning can take place that two important points may be forgotten: first, that some children come to school already having experienced failure in their learning – they need re-training and re-activating, however difficult that may be to achieve. Second, the teacher has to appreciate that, though all we have said about the match is relevant to early learning and to the later stages also, the child in school may need help in achieving this match.

Much of what is learned in school is artificial (not in the negative sense of the term) and technically complex. If the match is right, the child will want to learn, but he will often need help to see what there is to learn and how one may attack it. Bennett's research (1976) may well indicate that the so-called 'progressive' teacher is treading the same *laissez-faire* path as the nursery teacher at the next stage. Creating a child-centred environment in which learning can take place is important, but it is not the whole story. Learning demands structure and direction; not, as I have already said, an authoritarian and rigid structure, but a structure, nevertheless, which is achieved partly by being explicit about the functions of teaching. The pupil is entitled to be told the purpose of the suggested (or even imposed) activity; he needs to be provided with relevant information and help, both when he asks for it and when he is seen to need it. Skills (for example in phonic analysis) can be learned quite easily at an early age by most pupils, and there is no point in the teacher's holding them back — though she must not *force* them into formal work either. The teacher is also there to share enthusiasms and interests; for instance, the reading to pupils of stories, poems or other material which the teacher finds enjoyable and worthwhile can never be overdone. Such activities are worthwhile both for their own sake and as important models: they show the pupil what learning is for. Teachers who do not themselves read should not be surprised if their pupils do not do so either.

The idea of activities practised for their own sake can be taken much further. No school should ever teach children language or push a language programme without a constant awareness of what the language is for. Those who want their children to leave a class at the end of the year only as competent readers, rather than as children who have read valuable, interesting, informative books have missed part of the point. It is for this reason that both Blank (1973) and our own project work (Cashdan and Philps, 1977), although concerned entirely with the dialogue taking place between the teacher and the pupil, do not describe this dialogue as a 'language programme'. In fact, we have been concerned to develop the child's interest and ability in analysing, discussing, predicting and manipulating the world about him. Such a programme might best be described, perhaps, as a 'science programme'; inevitably it makes heavy use of language.

Good teachers try to teach *all* the children in their charge, but if they are not careful they will teach none of them. The capable pupils, who appreciate and share the school's aims, will learn without a teacher; the less 'advantaged' will not learn anyway. This would seem to suggest that the teacher might reach only a small, middle group. In fact, if, as I have suggested, the teacher can become a consultant, and yet not abdicate his or her role, such a pessimistic view will not have to be adopted. The teacher must constantly monitor her own effort and that of each of her pupils.

Conclusion — the goal

Although I was concerned earlier to question the assumptions of the educator, there can be no doubt that society *does* dictate much of what happens in school. It is for this reason that both the de-schooling movement and the extreme progressive wing in education experience difficulties, because they are trying to act as if they were outside a society to which they (and the children) in fact belong. I am advocating not a complete change of educational goals, but an explicit debate about them and an openness about what the teacher is trying to achieve with his/her pupils.

Such debate might provide an important stimulus for change. It seems to me that the school system needs to move much more in the direction of serving its clientele, rather than dictating to it. The school needs to be seen, by both pupils and parents, as a facility (for which they have paid) provided for their use. It is not, in my view, particularly healthy to think of the teacher as paid by an Education

Authority or some other such abstract body — ultimately, he is paid by the pupils and parents themselves and should see himself as running a shop in which he helps them choose wisely. The metaphor is a useful one — the shopkeeper stays in business only if he can persuade his customers to come a second time. Given the choice, how many of our 'customers' would use our schools again?

References

Bennett, N. (1976) *Teaching Style and Pupil Progress*. London: Open Books.

Bernstein, B. (1971 onwards) *Class, Codes and Control, Vols. I–III*. London: Routledge.

Blank, M. (1973) *Teaching Learning in the Preschool: A Dialogue Approach*. Columbus, Ohio: Charles Merrill.

Burt, C. (1937) *The Backward Child*. London: University of London Press.

Cashdan, A. and Philps, J. F. (1975) 'Nursery teachers' classroom behaviour in the light of their constructs of pupils: an exploratory study,' (Paper presented to the International Society for the Study of Behavioural Development, Guildford).

Cashdan, A. and Philps, J. F. (1977) 'Teaching style and pupil progress: the preschool period.' In *Studies in Reading*, Greaney, V., Ed. Dublin: Educational Company of Ireland.

Cazden, C. B. (1970) 'The neglected situation in child language and education.' In *Language and Poverty*, Williams, F., Ed. Chicago: Markham.

DES (1967) *Children and their Primary Schools* (The Plowden Report). London: HMSO.

DES (1975) *A Language for Life* (The Bullock Report). London: HMSO.

Douglas, J. W. B. (1964) *The Home and the School*. London: Macgibbon and Kee.

Edwards, A. D. (1976) *Language in Culture and Class*. London: Heinemann Educational.

Garner, J. and Bing, M. (1973) 'Inequalities of teacher-pupil contacts,' *British Journal of Educational Psychology, 43*, 234–43.

Goodacre, E. J. (1968) *Teachers and their Pupils' Home Background*. Slough: NFER.

Goodman, K. S. (1967) 'Reading: a psycholinguistic guessing game,' *Journal of the Reading Specialist, 6*, 126–35.

Hess, R. D. and Shipman, V. C. (1965) 'Early experience and the socialization of cognitive modes in children,' *Child Development, 36*, 869–86.

Hunt, J. McV. (1969) *The Challenge of Incompetence and Poverty*. Urbana, Illinois: University of Illinois Press.

Labov, W. (1969) 'The logic of nonstandard English,' In *Tinker, Tailor . . .* Keddie, N., Ed. Harmondsworth: Penguin Books (1973).

Pidgeon, D. A. (1970). *Expectation and Pupil Performance*. Slough: NFER.

Rosen, H. (1972) *Language and Class*. Bristol: Falling Wall Press.

Rosenthal, R. and Jacobson, L. (1968) *Pygmalion in the Classroom*. New York: Holt, Rinehart and Winston.

Swift, D. F. (1966) 'Social class and achievement motivation. *Educational Research, 8,* 83–95.

Trudgill, P. (1975) *Accent, Dialect and the School*. London: Edward Arnold.

Trevarthen, C. (1974) 'Conversations with a two-month old,' *New Scientist*, May 5th.

White, B. L., et al. (1973) *Experience and Environment: Major Influences on the Development of the Young Child, I*. Englewood Cliffs, New Jersey: Prentice-Hall.

Wiseman, S. (1964) *Education and the Environment*. Manchester: Manchester University Press.

2

Language in Education — a Linguistic Perspective

DAVID CRYSTAL

The discussion of language in education following in the wake of the Bullock Report has raised several overlapping and theoretically controversial linguistic themes, such as the desirability of linguistic screening for children held to be particularly 'at risk', and the choice of situations and materials felt to be appropriate for developing sensitivity to linguistic structure. In the last analysis, all such themes presuppose a common practical purpose: a concern to improve standards of language use in children. But in attempting to bridge the gap between theoretical debate and teaching practice, it is easy to underestimate the several kinds of linguistic knowledge that are needed. In fact, the aim of improving linguistic standards — which I take to be axiomatic — presupposes seven major stages, all of which relate to commonly-recognized educational tasks. These stages involve:

(a) identifying the specific linguistic problems in a sample of work of an individual child (or adult);
(b) describing the problematic features in a consistent and coherent manner;
(c) judging the typicality of these features for the child's language use as a whole (or as near to the whole as one can get); that is, classifying the problems into types;
(d) comparing individual children with respect to specific problems

and types; that is, ultimately establishing normative characteristics for groups;

(e) setting up a developmental scale in terms of which children can be rated;

(f) selecting immediate teaching goals, arising out of a comparison between target standard and attainment;

(g) devising and evaluating remedial techniques.

It will be evident that each stage presupposes the one(s) preceeding. There are no short cuts. Remediation (f,g) presupposes assessment (c,d,e), which presupposes identification of the existence of a problem (a,b). The surer our knowledge of the foundation stages, accordingly, the more confident subsequent pedagogical work will be. Which, then, are the weakest links in this chain of reasoning, and which stages can be most assisted by recent advances in linguistics?

It is usually assumed that (b), the need to master a terminology for the description of language, is a major problem facing any teacher wishing to investigate language problems systematically. It is certainly true that the precise use of technical terms is an invaluable aid to thinking, but learning *how* to describe is by no means the primary problem. Far more important is the need to be clear in one's mind as to exactly *what* the nature of the problem is. This is perhaps the most neglected of all the variables implicit in the list above, and yet it is pivotal. It is of little value to provide detailed techniques to facilitate (b), statistical techniques for (d), or language acquisitional scales for (e), if there is no agreement as to the end of the exercise. To what extent, therefore, *is* there agreement among teachers (or, for that matter, in society at large) that there is a problem? I am not referring here to a general sense of unease, which affects everyone, that 'standards' are deteriorating, but to the awareness of *specific* linguistic problems. To what extent would it be possible for a given group of teachers to agree that, for a given group of children, a specific set of linguistic difficulties constitutes the primary education problem? After this question is answered, we can then address the question of how far traditional techniques help in solving these problems, and how urgently new techniques are needed.

Localizing problems is, however, by no means straightforward. Addressing a given group of teachers and asking them to identify a 'top five' list of inadequacies that they would like to eradicate in their pupils' linguistic behaviour produces an extremely wide range of topics, and little agreement about priorities. Classifying reactions obtained in this way illustrates very well the range of interpretations given to the 'language' problem. The following discussion is based upon the replies of 200 teachers from the junior/middle school range.

1   Most teachers concentrated their remarks on their children's productive, rather than receptive use of language. Several concerned criticisms of pupils' inadequacies in writing and speaking. Hardly any reference was made to problems of reading comprehension; no reference at all was made to listening comprehension (in contrast with the emphasis given to this topic in the other branch of remedial linguistic training, speech therapy). On the other hand, several issues raised under the heading of *language* problems were, rather, *pre-language* problems — for example, poor memory, erratic attention, lack of confidence, or no imagination. These are all factors crucial for successful language development. However, it should be emphasized that they are not linguistic problems as such, and should not be confused with those difficulties which are susceptible to a specifically linguistic solution.

2   The majority of the reactions focused on what was actually there — the real or imagined errors in the child's use of language. Less attention was paid to what was *not* there; for example, the limitations on the child's expression, as viewed from the perspective of the teachers' experience of the desired level of children's language for that group. It is of course always more difficult to be confident and systematic about errors of omission than about errors of commission, and remarks were accordingly rather vague; for example, 'limited vocabulary', 'no development of ideas', and (a little more specifically) 'poor use of adjectives'. But both of these dimensions are essential for a complete assessment of a child's difficulties, and they should complement each other. It is particularly important to bear the existence of these two dimensions in mind in the primary age range, where the learning of several central features of the adult language is still going on. (The developing use of patterns of emphatic word order and of sentence connectivity is discussed below; see Crystal, 1976, Chapter 2.)

3   In concentrating on what was evident in a child's language, most teachers focussed on a particular sample of usage they had obtained, such as an essay, a taped dialogue, or a reading aloud

task. The theoretical limitations of such sampling were generally appreciated, but on the whole the features selected for comment were presented for discussion without reference to the characteristics of the particular sample used. Yet to label a linguistic feature an 'error', without further qualification, can be highly misleading. At least the three following distinctions should be taken into account.

First, one should ask, with reference to one's sample, whether the language feature in question has been used consistently or inconsistently throughout. If the former, is the feature consistently correct or incorrect? The diagnostic value of this question is significant. One assumes that consistently correct usage denotes acquisition, and that consistently incorrect usage denotes the opposite. Absence of structures proves very little — it may suggest significant lack of ability, or there may be a sampling limitation. But inconsistent usage is potentially important. Both in speech and writing, areas of inconsistency show the linguistic features currently being acquired by the child, and suggest the need for extra attention. For example, one child wrote: *The man broke his arm because he fell off the ladder and his foot slipped.* The teacher had corrected *and* to *when*. What is the error? On the face of it, two interpretations suggest themselves: over-use of *and*; inadequate command of the use of *when*. Looking elsewhere in this child's work, neither explanation seemed to hold up. The child did sometimes over-use *and*, but only when long strings of events were being described. He was also able to write such sentences as *They went home when it was tea-time*. This leaves one further possibility — that the problem has arisen because of the structural complexity of the sentence which contains a main clause with two subordinate clauses of different semantic types. It may be that a child can cope with one main clause plus one subordinate clause, and get the right conjunction, the right sequence of tenses, and so on; but when faced with two subordinate clauses, he finds the second one difficult to process, and thus opts for 'and' as the easiest way out. 'At least this way (he might reason), I can get in the relevant fact (that the foot slipped) and this is a move in the right direction, in expressing what I want to say.'

This explanation is plausible, for children do have difficulty developing control over the range and sequencing of subordinate clause types (see, e.g., Clark, 1973; French & Brown, 1977) and this process is by no means complete for speech by the time a child gets to school. It is therefore highly unlikely that a great deal of control would manifest itself in the written medium. And one would expect to find, in the work of this child, a range of similar errors as he experimented with various combinations of clause types. One would at least have to look elsewhere in his work before one could decide on the significance of the error in the example given above.

In short, this example illustrates a general principle: that description of the *whole* sample of work must precede any evaluation of the child's linguistic ability. A natural tendency is to see an error at the beginning of a piece of written work, and to mark it as such; but how serious the error is, and what kind of constructive comment to write in the margin, will only emerge once one has seen a particular error in relation to other instances of its use and with reference to relevant process of language acquisition.

A second distinction, a prerequisite for a clear discussion of the notion of 'error', is that between impossibility and undesirability. An error may be *impossible*, in the sense that no natural dialect of English uses it, or *undesirable*, in that it breaks some real or imagined sociolinguistic or stylistic norm. Teacher reaction varied widely on this point, reflecting traditional controversy. For some, traditional shibboleths, such as split infinitives, ranked highly as errors; for others, these were of little consequence as long as intelligibility remained. Other aspects of undesirability related to an inspecific notion of frequency. Over-use of *'and'* in written work was one of the most commonly cited errors, but there was considerable difference of opinion as to how many instances of 'and' constituted an acceptable string.

Third, one should bear in mind the fact that the gravity of a large number of errors can be established only in the light of what the child intended to say or write. But it is very rarely the case that the adult view of what constitutes an appropriate use of language is checked by explicitly referring to the intuitions of the child. The practical and theoretical problems involved in discovering a child's intentions are very great, of course; but these should not blind us to the possibility that sometimes we may be considering as inadequate a use of language which was a deliberate choice on the child's part, and which he might have been able to justify, given the chance. Ambiguous usage is the crux of the problem. In the sentence (used in the essay analysed below) *She sat down looking at her cards*, several teachers corrected *looking* to *to look*, though whether this is the right thing to do clearly depends on what was meant. But it is not solely a matter of ambiguity. It must not be forgotten that the distance between an adult's and a child's language is still quite marked at age 10, especially as regards their relative awareness of vocabulary, figurative language, etc. (see Gardner *et al.*, 1975). One must therefore always be aware of the danger of seeing a child's usage as poor, by adult standards, whereas in fact it may be advanced, or innovative, when judged in its own terms.

4   Beneath this last distinction lies the contrast between the two main dimensions of linguistic analysis: language *use* and language *structure*. Distinguishing clearly between these dimensions is fundamental in any application of linguistic ideas, but in the present case the two were frequently confused. Under the heading of language use, one is referring to the choice of a particular style or dialect on the part of a child, and therefore to his sense of linguistic appropriateness. Examples of 'errors' here would be the use of local dialect forms, or informal constructions such as contractions in formal written contexts where the standard language is required. As has frequently been pointed out in recent years (e.g., Trudgill 1975; Crystal 1976), the use of dialect or informal language may be appropriate on other occasions. Rather, one should develop an awareness of the coexistence of several different varieties of language within a community, and aim to instil in the child a functional command of them. It was nonetheless common to see in the present exercise the assumed existence of a single standard of correctness, 'errors' being identified without regard to the context in which the language was used. The dangers that this attitude gives rise to have been well discussed (e.g., by Doughty *et al.*, 1971; Martin *et al.*, 1976), so I will not go into them here. Errors 'common to children and their parents' were listed by one teacher, and this heading summarizes well the underlying misconception.

Particularly important with reference to language use, especially in the early school period, is the contrast between the language demands and expectations of the school and those of the home. It is axiomatic that one should build in school on the foundations of what the child already has, but it is by no means uncommon to see building going ahead with no systematic cognizance being taken of what is already there. The following topic area provides an example.

In written work, one of the most common criticisms was a child's failure to complete sentences, or his omission of important information such as the subject of the sentence, or an adverbial (e.g., *'when* did the event take place?'), or his use of ambiguous pronouns '(Who does the *he* refer to?'). But we must not forget how distinctive the written language is in its sentence construction, and how great the distance is between most styles of writing and conversational speech, which provides the norm of our linguistic consciousness. Colloquial speech is generally in dialogue form, for example; hence the child is used to responding to others' stimuli while he is communicating, thus producing elliptical constructions; for example, *To the library* said in response to *Where are you going?* In colloquial speech, too, the subject is frequently omitted, because it is obvious to whom the action refers when the speaker and listener share the same context; for example, *Having a nice time?*, *Got a new car!* The ever-present context makes several linguistic features redundant, and promotes in particular the frequent use of *deictic* words (words that point directly to features of the non-linguistic world), such as *this, that, here, there* or *one.* Whole sentences can be totally context-bound in this way; for example, *And so she did, That one does too.* These are some of the features that characterize the economy and fluency of conversational speech; they would obviously be out of place in most kinds of writing. But given the fact that children are well-versed in their use, being fluent users of informal speech, it is not at all surprising that these features will emerge in their early attempts to master the rules of the written language.

An important bridging operation on the teacher's part, accordingly, is to bring home to the child how independent of context the written language tends to be, and how important it is for the writer to be aware of the demands placed upon him by the varying situations in which written communication is appropriate (cf. Martin *et al.,* 1976). But the theoretical issue here is not restricted to the task of learning to write. If one takes the example of 'incomplete' sentences mentioned above, one finds that it needs to be considered with reference to both speech and writing. Most children have a colloquial speech background which involves a predominance of multiply-coordinated constructions of the kind illustrated in Crystal (1976, Chapter 1), with a high frequency of *and*s and filler clauses, such as *you know.*

If there have been no external forces disciplining their thinking (as with, say, parents using the Ladybird pre-reading books), then there could well be difficulties in teaching such children the standard notion of a 'complete' sentence. Under such circumstances, a great deal of cognitive foundation may need to be laid before one can satisfactorily proceed to such notions, whether in the written language or in speech. This problem faces all teachers in their initial assessment of error: is the incompleteness a linguistic or a prelinguistic difficulty for the child?

5   The great majority of teacher responses, however, came under the heading of language structure, and here the need to use a linguistic model capable of classifying the diverse reactions was apparent. Using the model presented in previous work (Crystal, 1976), the comments could be grouped readily into three areas, and sub-classified:

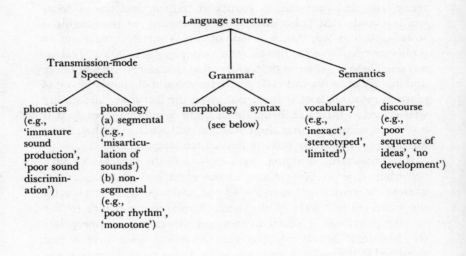

A further classification of stated errors, based on this model, was also useful:

> A *single level* problem is solely one of spelling *or* syntax *or* vocabulary
> etc., for example, *john* for a proper name, *January, Peter threw the ball on
> the floor* (where 'dropped' is the required meaning). A *multi-level* error is
> more complex, involving problems at two or more levels; for example:
> spelling + vocabulary, for example, *The bare ate him*; vocabulary +
> grammar, for example, *all ready* for *already, after Sue went out* (where
> 'afterwards' was expected); spelling + grammar (a rare combination),
> for example, *its / it's   their / they're / there, could of*; vocabulary +
> punctuation (a rare combination), for example, *Mr, Mister. Jones*;
> spelling+vocabulary+grammar, for example, *It is to early.*

The important point here is that, whereas most people assume that
errors are identifiable at one level of language structure only, the
majority of errors in a piece of work involve more than one, with
consequent problems of analysis and exposition in remediation.

6   The majority of teachers' *complaints* about language came
under the heading of grammar. This is not surprising. Grammar is
the organizing principle of language, within which vocabulary,
sounds and spellings are organized into meaningful units. Because of
its basic role, accordingly, some further classification of errors, into
the main types of grammatical problem posed, is urgent.[1] In fact,
five areas of grammatical structure seem particularly important: (a)
sentence-sequencing; (b) sentence structure; (c) clause structure;
(d) phrase structure; (e) word structure. Typical comments were:

(a) 'loose connection of ideas', 'poor paragraphing', 'the sentences
    come out in any order';
(b) 'poor sequence of tenses', 'incomplete sentences', 'poor clause
    development';
(c) 'bad word order', for example, *'hardly he had come'*;
(d) 'limited' phrases, for example, 'no use of adjectives';
(e) 'confused word-endings', such as *-ed* and *-ing*.

---

[1]One should note here the contrast between a linguistic orientation to grammatical
work and the aims of traditional parsing and clause analysis. The present approach
never treats the analysis of language in the classroom as an end in itself, merely to
develop a mastery of terminology. The primary aim is to analyse in order to assess
and thus develop ability. Consequently, no language analysis should ever take place
until one has first established the nature of the language problem which has given rise
to it, and has a subsequent remedial aim in mind (see below).

A useful way of illustrating the various stages listed at the beginning of this paper is to take one of these areas and look at the issues that emerge in constructing a remedial programme. In a recent discussion-group, involving mainly teachers of 9–10 year-olds, it was finally agreed that area (a) was a particular problem. As one teacher put it, wearily: 'With several in my class, one could take their story, cut out each sentence, shuffle the sentences and "deal" a new story, and the result would be no better and no worse than the first effort!' Identification of a problem, the first stage discussed at the beginning of this chapter, was achieved.

The second stage was deciding how to describe these features. It was felt likely that the means the children used to connect their sentences was inadequate. Unfortunately, traditional handbooks do not pay much attention to this problem[2] though it has come to the fore in recent descriptions of English (as in Quirk *et al.*, 1972, Chapter 10; Halliday and Hasan, 1976). Consequently, it was necessary to spend some time establishing what the potential of the language is, as far as sentence connectivity is concerned. Before one can establish what is missing in a child's language, one must first know precisely what could have been there. Accordingly, it was asked: How many kinds of sentence connectivity are there in English? *A Grammar of Contemporary English* (Quirk *et al.*, 1972) shows that there are four main grammatical means:

(1) By no explicit marker, symbolized as S/S (S = Sentence): For example, when one uses a series of parallel structures, the very use of parallelism causes one to see the sentences as working together to communicate a particular meaning, as with a string of rhetorical questions in a political speech, or a series of italicised lines in a written text.

(2) The use of a linking word: $S \times S$. Here, two types are possible:

(a) A time/place word; for example, *here, there, then, earlier, already* .... The connectivity function of such words is clear if one tries to start an utterance with one: *'Then John came in'* can hardly be one's opening remark.

(b) Logical connectors, such as *and, or, but,* and the various

---

[2]Grammatical features are not the only ones which connect sentences, of course; other semantic or situational features may, as in: *The Prime Minister . . . Mr. Callaghan . . .*, or *He died . . . He was buried.* Graphic layout, such as in official forms, may also connect groups of sentences. The point made above is that the fewer the grammatical clues to the organization of a text, the more difficult it will be to understand, as more has to be 'read in' by the text user.

related words that reinforce their meanings, such as *moreover, however, actually*. One should note here the several underlying senses of a word like *and*, embracing such diverse meanings in a sentence as *X happened and Y happened*. The sense may be result (*and* = 'and therefore'), chronology (*and* = 'and then', as in so much story-telling), or addition (*and* = 'and also', as in a great deal of descriptive writing), as well as other things.

(3) The use of a replacement: *x* in sentence 1 is replaced by *y* in sentence 2 (*S* / *S*). The total substitution of a stretch of

$$\overset{\downarrow}{x} \to \overset{\downarrow}{y}$$

language by a word may be symbolized by *y*. The best examples are the pronouns (*he, she*, etc.) or words such as *do, so* and *one*. *y* may also be the partial repetition of a phrase, as in the anaphoric (i.e., backwards-referring) use of the definite article, for example, *the boy* presupposes a previously mentioned *boy*, whereas *a boy* does not.

(4) Deletion: *x* in sentence 1 is omitted in sentence 2 (viz. *s*   *s*).

$$\overset{\downarrow}{x} \to \overset{\downarrow}{-}$$

There are also two types here: *ellipsis* is the absence of part of a sentence, which thereby shows the dependence of that sentence on some other sentence, for example, *To town*, following *Where are you going?*; *comparison* makes it quite clear from the form of the sentence used that a contrast is being made with something previously stated or understood, as in *That's bigger*.

In theory, then, one can see how sentence-connectivity can go wrong:

(1) There may be no explicit connectivity at all, and no parallelism of structure to justify its absence (*S* / *S* / *S* / *S*...)

(2) Only some types of connectivity may be used. Usually parts of types (2) and (3) above are used, but with significant omissions (see below).

(3) Some types may be over-used, especially:
   (a) over-use of *and, then,* etc.;
   (b) over-use of pronouns as subject.

If we now look at a sample of a child's writing, it is possible to use this framework to locate the main areas of probable difficulty for an individual child — the classificatory stage (c) referred to on page 1. The following essay was produced by a nine-year-old.

Kim B   26th November   The Birthday present 1976

This is a story about a girl called Sue. It was her birthday today and
she was looking forward to it because she was getting a brand new pair
of roller skates from her uncle. She sat down looking at her cards. Then
a knock at the door made Sue jump She was hoping that it was her
uncle but it was her friend already for the party but she said "It is to
early". "Im very sorry Ill come later on okay bye." Then a glance
caught her eye her uncle was across the road he had a parcel in his
arms. Sue ran to him "Happy Birthday" Sam he said and she gave him
a big kiss. A present was given to her. She quickly ran indoors and
opend the box and there she saw a brand new pair of skates. They were
red with white laces, She asked her uncle to do up her laces and he said
"yes" So after Sue went roller skating. She even tried to do tricks but
she was only a learner. She skated down a hill and her laces were not
tight enough and she fell and her skates went into a dump yard. She
began to cry on the way home. and thinking what her (grandad) uncle
would say. She didn't go in until her uncle was gone and after that he
was gone she crept in and ran upstairs and protended to put the roller
skates away. Her mum said "did your skates go okay"? "Yes." "Did
you know it is Christmas tomorrow"? "No." "Mum if I tell you something will promise not to tell uncle"? "Yes." "I lost my skates". Well ill
lett you what I shall get you a pair for christmas exsacly the same. and
so she did, And uncle came over and he said "how are your roller
skates"? "Very lovely thankyou!" anyway Im inviting you all to dinner
today "horay". Can I bring my roller skates"? "Of course", and Sue
was very happy.

The two main characteristics of connectivity in this essay are
obvious: the use of *and* to the apparent exclusion of other forms of
connectivity, and the highly frequent pronominal role. The
obviousness of these remarks hides some complexities, however, to
which I referred earlier. Why *should* the child resort to these
strategies? In both cases, investigating the most noticeable features
leads us into other areas, and suggests explanations for the
difficulties that could tie in with the child's linguistic behaviour as a
whole. Perhaps this is a child who is having difficulty in mastering
the more complex subordinating conjunctions of the language, or in
building sentences using non-finite clauses (evidenced by *She began to
cry on the way home. and thinking what her uncle would say.*). Both of these
structures are relatively late language acquisitional features.
Perhaps the child views *and* as particularly appropriate for certain

kinds of expression, suggesting an attempt at stylistic contrast — the way in which the construction to some degree reflects the speed of events in *She skated down a hill and her laces were not tight enough and she fell and her skates went into a dump yard.* Perhaps it is the system of logical connectivity itself that gives the child difficulty (as shown by the second *but* in *but it was her friend already for the party but she said 'It is to early . . .').* It is plain that the child has begun to control aspects of these areas of grammar (as indicated by the use of *because . . ., looking at . . ., even . . ., until . . .,* etc.), but the systems of contrasts involved have clearly not been completely acquired.

Similarly, one can look at the pronoun usage, and draw inferences about acquisition. Here the issue is not this child's learning of the actual pronominal items, but the relationship of the pronouns to other parts of the sentence. In the sentence *Then a knock at the door made Sue jump,* given that *Sue* is the only subject engaged in actions at this point, a pronoun would be expected. The learning of constructions involving double pronouns, identity of reference of pronouns, and related matters, however, comes relatively late in language acquisition (cf. contrasts such as *John gave a book to Jim, and he gave one to Mary* and *John gave a book to Jim, and HE gave one to Mary,* which are still being acquired in speech by many children at age 9; cf. Chomsky, 1969).

One might also note here the related problem of ambiguity, where *but she said* could refer to either Sue or the friend. And perhaps one might reflect on the pervasive stylistic monotony of the pronoun constructions. What happens when a pronoun is used as a subject of a sentence in English? All the 'weight' of the sentence comes after the verb. This is in fact the natural order of things in English speech (cf. Quirk *et al.,* 1972, Chapter 14). This feature can readily be recognized when one compares the greater naturalness of *It's nice to see you digging the garden,* to *To see you digging the garden is nice.* In a developed style, one introduces variations in focus and theme to avoid monotonous concentration on the object and subject of the sentence. In speech, too, one uses intonational emphasis to avoid monotony. In Kim's essay, however, apart from a certain mobility in the use of *he said,* there is no thematic variation; the subjects are short and repetitive. The one clear attempt to break out of this pattern is worth singling out: the use of the passive in *A present was given to her.* This would generally be a rather artificial construction at this point — though whether the child intended the formality, impersonality, or pomposity that attends the use of the passive is unknowable. It would have been far easier to have written *She got a present, He gave her a present*, or the like, but because of the thematic variation it is a quite exciting move in the right direction. Once again, there are signs of acquisition in progress.

In trying to establish the typical errors in this child's work, it should be noted that we have had to make use of assumptions relating to stages (d) and (e) in the teaching process referred to on the first page of this chapter. In particular, we have noted that both the problem areas discussed — complex sentence construction and thematic variation — are aspects of language that tend to be acquired relatively late, between 5 and 10 years of age. Of course, the most important implication of this is that the problem this child faces may not solely be one with the written language. It is crucial for the teacher to check on this possibility, as there is little point in introducing remedial written work if the child has had no experience of the constructions in question in his reading, or, more fundamentally, in his speaking or listening comprehension. For specific areas of construction, the point should be easy enough to check.

Let us take, as an example, the use of sentence-connecting adverbials, such as *actually, fortunately, happily, later, in fact*. These might be absent in a child's written output (as in the essay above). A look through the main reading materials used by the child would show fairly quickly whether such patterns were being regularly used. (One could note, in this respect, the sentence-by-sentence progression of several traditional reading schemes which jump, suddenly and without a control in complexity, to paragraphs of story-text involving quite complex connectives. In *Skylarks*, on the other hand, building in gradual increases in the complexity of sentence linkage is a main feature; cf. Bevington and Crystal, 1975). It would be more difficult to check on the child's use of such connectives in spontaneous speech and listening comprehension, but a relatively easy matter to check on this in controlled situations. The teacher might write a list of adverbials on the board, then begin to read a sentence, requiring the children to continue it using one of the adverbials. For example, with *happily, quickly, fortunately* on the board:

Teacher: *Yesterday, we went to town. Fortunately, . . .*
Child: *Fortunately, it wasn't raining.*

Remedial attention to this problem might continue using variants of the *Find a Story* or *Roll a Story* materials (Vidler, 1974), where one can 'ring the changes' on a sentence by systematically varying the connecting link, with varying results ranging from the incongruous to the absurd. One may even find story material in print that focusses on the remedial feature (as in Charlip, 1964, for the entertaining contrast between *fortunately* and *unfortunately*), but rather more often one would have to work up some simple materials of one's own. In this way, the diagnosis of writing → reading → speaking → comprehension can be reversed; comprehension and speech exercises lead to reading patterns compatible with speaking ability and thence to promoting their use in the written language. The sentence-maker techniques in *Breakthrough to Language* are examples of this process.

Selecting immediate teaching goals and devising remedial techniques, described as stages (f) and (g) at the beginning of the chapter, go closely together in practice. There is little point in setting oneself a goal if there are no practicable techniques available for reaching it. But with ingenuity it is usually possible to devise a strategy for attacking any structural linguistic problem and, moreover, for doing so in an entertaining way. The children who laugh at Charlip's *Fortunately* . . ., or who construct more and more fantastic story-boards, little realize that they are being drilled in 'sentence-connecting adverbials'. It is also a far cry from the traditional approaches of formal grammar, where one learned the structures (and the terminology) first, and thought what to do about them afterwards. The kind of background knowledge that is required of the teacher before he can lead his children in this direction is, however, quite considerable, as I hope this paper has shown. It is no greater than that which has to be mastered in order to implement several other areas of expertise within the profession; but because it has been so neglected, the problem, perhaps, seems larger than it is. Group discussion of the problems, especially in schools, can be of great value in bringing the issues into perspective. Supported by a small amount of judicious reading and a willingness to experiment, it is remarkable how quickly the bridge between theory and practice in educational linguistic work can be constructed.

References

Bevington, J. and Crystal, D. (1975) *Skylarks*. London: Nelson.

Charlip, R. (1964) *Fortunately*. New York: Parents' Magazine Press.

Chomsky, C. (1969) *The Acquisition of Syntax in Children from Five to Ten*. Cambridge, Mass: MIT Press.

Clark, E. V. (1973) 'How children describe time and order,' in *Studies of Child Language Development*. Ferguson, C. and Slobin, D. I., Eds. New York: Holt, Rinehart and Winston.

Crystal, D. (1976) *Child Language, Learning, and Linguistics*. London: Edward Arnold.

Doughty, P., Pearce, J. and Thornton, G. (1971) *Language in Use:* London: Edward Arnold.

French, L. A., and Brown, A. L. (1977) 'Comprehension of *before* and *after* in logical and arbitrary sequences,' *Journal of Child Language, 4*.

Gardner, H., Kircher, M., Winner, E. and Perkins, D. (1975) 'Children's metaphoric productions and preferences,' *Journal of Child Language, 2*, 125–41.

Halliday, M. A. K. and Hasan, R. (1976) *Cohesion in English*. London: Longman.

Martin, N., D'Arcy, P., Newton, B. and Parker, R. (1976) *Writing and Learning Across the Curriculum 11-16*. London: Ward Lock Educational.

Quirk, R., Greenbaum, S., Leech, G. N. and Svartvik, J. (1972) *A Grammar of Contemporary English*. London: Longman.

Trudgill, P. (1975) *Accent, Dialect, and the School*. London: Edward Arnold.

Vidler, M. (1974) *Find a Story*. Harmondsworth: Penguin Books.

3

Reading — an Integrated Methodology

GEOFFREY ROBERTS

Considerable confusion (to both teachers and pupils) has been caused in the teaching of reading because many British teachers have followed their text books on the acquisition of reading skills in a segmented manner, and have transposed this approach into an equally segmented practical programme. They have consequently regarded the teaching of reading as the transmission of a hierarchical order of skills, each skill necessarily preceding the others in chronological order. The result is a piece-meal approach by many writers and teachers, one that has left the child to synthesize unaided a fragmented set of sub-skills, while the teaching has stressed only one element at a time, such as learning the letters, identification of words, or comprehending prose.

Nothing could be more likely to give the learner a fragmented view of reading, because, although hierarchical order of skills can be identified theoretically, in practice these skills constantly impinge upon each other from the very beginning of the process of learning to read. From the moment that a child first sees the text, he begins to react positively by constructing thoughts · about the emerging message. The child cannot obliterate from his mind speculations about the ensuing meaning while concentrating upon the identification of the sounds of letters and words. If this did happen, then the massive burden of interpreting the phonic complexity of English spelling without the help of the additional cues provided by the meaning of the passage would annihilate any meaning that letter and word identification may have had for a child during the early stages of learning to read.

The letter-based approaches, both alphabetic and phonic, regarded the acquisition of a knowledge of individual letter-sound correspondences as a sufficient basis upon which the learner could acquire the skills of reading. The word-based approaches went a little further, from the realization of the place of individual letters within words to the more radical idea that the string of letters was the effective and critical unit of language for the purpose of word identification. None of these approaches, however, took into consideration the simple fact that the arrangement of words in relation to one another can critically affect their meaning and, furthermore, that even this word order may not always be enough to ensure understanding. It is the arrangement of words that gives meaning to *The boy bit the dog*, whereas the two sentences *John is easy to please* and *John is eager to please*, although similar in structure, have John as the recipient in one and as the initiator in the other. Hence there is a third major approach to reading, first expressed in the writings of Huey and Thorndike, and later in those of Goodman and Smith. This regards phono-graphemic and lexical cues as no more important than the syntactic and semantic cues embedded in the phrase, sentence or even larger segment of the text.

This dichotomy between the segmented and the global view of learning to read has continued to persist, because some teachers tend to take a simplistic view of the acquisition of the sub-skills of reading, seeing the task as the acquisition of sounds from a text rather than the interpretation of a text in terms of all the relevant information that is provided. They think, with some justification, that sounds will be associated with meaning. However, this view of reading is as limited and constrained as one that regards the skills of the brick-layer as sufficient to produce a building. Reading is not merely a matter of adding one 'learning brick' uniformly to another. The question of stress becomes crucial at a certain point in the construction of each surface. Similarly, in learning to read, phonological cues are inadequate to convey the meaning of such words as *tears*. They will take the learner so far as deciding that the word could be /tɛəz/ or /tiəz/, but the ultimate choice will depend upon syntactic and semantic cues obtained from the text in which the word stands: *The girl had tears in her eyes/dress*. Just as the architect evaluates the forces of stress, so the reader interprets the effects of the structure of the text upon meaning, and unless he does this he will not get meaning from what he reads; he will get merely sounds that may suggest idiosyncratic pieces of information, which may or may not add up to the message of the text. And unless the reader is getting a message that makes immediate sense to him, he will be confused, and this confusion can occur in terms of the use of any or all of the three categories of cues used in the interpretation of texts: semantic, syntactic and phono-graphemic. Furthermore, confusion in one category can lead to confusion in another: the sentence, *Does live in a whole in the ground*, if begun with the mistaken response /dəz/ (as in *He does the shopping*) could be subsequently ratified by a child with a Lancashire accent assuming that the syntax of written language corresponded exactly with that of his dialect, so that the sentence was transformed into a question, *Does (do you) live in a hole in the ground*?

The actual teaching of reading, in contrast with the discussion of the learning processes, should *not* be segmented into exclusive sub-skill training. Where sub-skills are to be taught, they should be practised within the context of the complete skill; letters should not be taught except within words, words should always appear within sentences, and, wherever possible, sentences should be part of a unitary passage. Only in this way can confusion be avoided or contained, so that one mistake does not lead to another, and so that an array of cues can act as a check upon the response to any particular cue. The child with a Lancashire accent would be alerted to his mistake in reading the sentence, *Does live in a hole . . .*, if that sentence was seen to be part of a text about the habits of female rabbits.

Many teachers, erroneously thinking that the interpretation of a text for meaning emanated solely from phonic responses, have regarded reading aloud as the principal, and in some cases the exclusive, activity in this interpretive process. Such a view ignores the fact that what is written is only an indication, and not necessarily an exact representation, of what is thought. This is manifest in the difference between deep and surface structure; the deep structure is what the author thinks and the surface structure is how he presents it in writing. Too great an emphasis on phonetics ignores the fact that the extraction of meaning from a text is more than taking the sum total of the sounds represented by the print. This over-simplified view of reading is represented in diagramatic

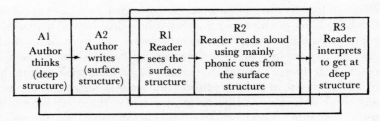

Figure **3.1**

form in Figure 3.1.

It can be seen that those who accept Figure 3.1 as representative of reading regard the phonic representation of the text as the major interpretative activity at the output stage; that is, reading aloud is the expression of the reader's interpretation of the text. Unfortunately, this takes the reader only to the surface structures and does not necessarily extract the meaning actually intended by the author. That may or may not come at the next stage, provided there is another stage. Unfortunately, many teachers allow the process of interpretation to stop at the point where the text is read aloud. The diagram also demonstrates the tremendous strain placed upon the new reader's knowledge of letter-sound correspondences and phonic skill and on his ability to make instantaneous adjustments to get the intonation necessary to bring sense out of sound.

An alternative approach, advocated in this chapter, is based upon the diagramatic sequence in Figure 3.2. In this diagram, R2/R3 is a stage in which the child uses all the cues at his disposal. He may utter some vocal responses to parts of the text, but his main objective is not to produce a sequence of sounds corresponding to the written symbols. It is to organize and re-organize his thoughts as he reacts tentatively to phonic, syntactic and semantic cues as they impinge upon each other. Hence, reading for meaning and reading aloud sequentially are seen as two separate things: the ultimate aim is to interpret the deep structure by means of the surface structure, and this may involve some vocal responses as part of a more complex response. Reading aloud is concerned primarily with the vocal reproduction of the surface structure. R4 is the stage that follows the interpretation of meaning and reverts to a reproduction of the surface structure.

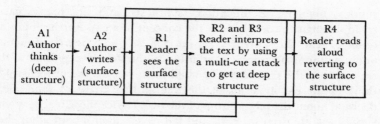

Figure **3.2**

This analysis suggests that the normal practice of starting to teach children to read using the model illustrated by Figure 3.1 should be abandoned, and that in its place should be an approach that trains children from the beginning to adopt the broad strategies they will subsequently use as readers (Figure 3.2). While they will not be able to act in every detail as competent readers, they will be experiencing a training in behaviour closely resembling their ultimate behaviour as readers, and not one that they will soon need to abandon as they develop reading skills.

Learning to read does not precede comprehension; they are both part of the same process. From the outset, the aim of the teacher should be to go beyond mere word calling and to get a response from the reader that indicates his understanding. Children must be alerted to the fact that what they already know contributes to their understanding of what they read. They must also be sufficiently flexible in their approach to a text to be willing to convert what is written into a form of language which they easily understand and remember. Thus the development of comprehension skills does not depend, in practice, on an innate ability to answer questions. Children must be taught and trained to use all the cues available — semantic, syntactic and phonological — and to manipulate the language in order to extract the full meaning from it.

It is clear from common experience that children do not find it difficult to learn the names and sounds of letters; neither is it beyond the capacity of the vast majority to learn a list of words by heart. On the other hand, many children are not able to use this knowledge and apply it in a way that will enable them to read. More is involved than the mere identification of each letter sound as a discrete entity in order to read the word *cat*. The process of the summation of these sounds involves modification, synthesis and in many cases re-adjustment to comply with the concept of a cat. Furthermore, in order to read the sentence, *The cat is in the tree*, a degree of mental organization is necessary in addition to the mere recognition of the six words in the sentence. The child must possess the propensity to think of the cat in terms of the tree and to arrive at some clear decision about the relationship of the two. Hence those teachers who simply ask children to read, and fail to ask them about what they have read, are failing to ensure that young readers go beyond the mechanical identification of letters and word sounds so that they can begin to interpret the sense of those sounds.

The purpose of this chapter, therefore, is to outline a programme of teaching in which the major parts of the complete skill of reading are clarified in ways suited to the learner, the task and the general organizational features of classrooms. Bartlett (1947) regarded an overview of a skill as essential in the acquisition of the components of that skill, so that the learner might gain some notion of his ultimate behavioural objectives as a learner, and Reid's research (1966) suggested that many children entering school did not have an overview of the activity called reading.

Now in order for children to obtain a vague idea of the process of communication through print, it is not enough merely to show them books and texts. These are the end products, and they give no indication to the uninitiated of how they are constructed — it is only through insight into how written language is constructed that the child can begin to realize what is required of the reader. Everyday experience suggests that we gain insights into any process more rapidly if we participate actively in that process than if we merely observe, because in all observation there is a tendency towards passivity and eventual loss of attention, especially in cases where the process is partially beyond immediate understanding. This fact is particularly relevant in the case of five-year-old children, whose cognitive functioning is on the whole intuitive and does not permit involved analytical behaviour.

At this stage, the child has a strong inclination to concentrate upon his immediate and specific activities; he has difficulties in analysis (Roberts, T., 1975); and words, so far as he is aware of them, are object-based. Thus, the teacher who wishes to inculcate some overview of reading in order to set the scene for the later stage of word and text analysis will need to devise a method or a series of teaching techniques that will clarify the issues for the child by allowing him to participate in the composition and construction of written English in ways that are commensurate with his mental capacities. This means that the framework of the text must centre upon something that is engaging the child's attention and involving him in actions at that moment. If he is an urban working-class child in a classroom full of exciting activity which he finds relevant and worthy of attention, then it seems a waste of the teacher's efforts to try to transpose him arbitrarily into a middle-class suburban garden or to a farm in the depths of the country! The modern British infant classroom provides ample opportunities for the child to become engrossed in some activity that may be followed immediately by the composition of a text based upon that activity. Furthermore, the young child can be encouraged to 'write' the text in his own words. Normally, this would be an impossible task but for the fact that there is now on the market a scheme that consists of a word bank of separate word cards (Mackay *et al.*, 1970), which may be used by the teacher to reconstruct in print the story or information related by the child. Later, the teacher may transcribe into the child's personal story book the text formulated from the child's speech.

However, let us not skip too quickly over this production of the child's story without noting the opportunities for discussion about the form and nature of what the child has said. For example, the child may cry, 'Me knee's bleeding', and the teacher will then provide the word cards corresponding to the written form, 'My knee is bleeding', and thereby begin to alert the child to the ways in which written English corresponds to and differs from the spoken forms.

After going over the sentence several times, and not too obtrusively pointing to some of the words, the teacher may transpose the statement into her own observation, 'Johnny's knee's bleeding' and its equivalent in the written form of, *Johnny has a bleeding knee*, and elicit in speech the written form 'I have a bleeding knee' from the child, thus demonstrating the connection in use between a proper noun and a pronoun without having to use any terminology whatsoever to describe her action; she thereby demonstrates the variability of the verb, similarly without reference to the grammatical action. The opportunities for language control at a stage when the child is virtually unaware of what he is doing are enormous, and yet he is being gently inducted into the process of the creation of written language. Vygotsky (1962) spoke of the gap between a child's written and spoken language. The word-card language-experience approach goes a considerable way towards closing that gap, and at the same time provides a basis for future insights into the structure of written language.

Furthermore, while bringing the content of the text closer to the child's immediate preoccupations and, at the same time, bringing that text into closer comparison with the sentence patterns used in speech by both child and teacher this method may be the only feasible way for the teacher to demonstrate, through the more concrete and active form of writing, those developments or alterations in speech that are possible for children at this early stage. By means of a thoughtful re-arrangement or substitution of the word cards when using the sentence maker in the *Breakthrough to Literacy* scheme, enabling children to see what is being done as well as hearing a different way of saying what needs to be said, it is possible that more significant results can be obtained than those obtained from the various published programmes for speech development, the effectiveness of which was questioned in the Bullock Report (DES, 1975).

In any case, a policy of teaching a child to become increasingly aware of the differences between written and spoken English, through his own participation in the manipulation of these differences, may effectively produce the 'set' for diversity necessary to cope with language patterns in books that differ from familiar patterns in his normal speech. This would then make unnecessary the dubious and generally unsatisfactory practice, introduced in some recent primers, of attempting to reproduce children's speech patterns into substantial parts of the text other then where direct speech is being reported (Roberts, 1977).

Having undergone a period of general induction into the interpretation of texts, with the word as the minimum unit under consideration and with emphasis on language patterns, the learner must begin to use phonological cues. The main units in terms of behaviour are letter and word discrimination and identification. In developing letter discrimination we cannot assume that young children at the outset see the differences between letters (see Gibson, 1965); Smith (1971) has suggested that children need to make comparisons in their own ways and to discover the significant differences between letters. In practice this has been the object of such references by teachers to *a* 'with a stalk' in *apple*, *k* 'looks like tall sister /k/, or 'kicking /k/', and *c* as 'fat baby /k/'. By using references like these, the teachers were calling attention to the idiosyncratic features of letter forms. Further guidance on this was given by Pick (1965), who suggests that similar letters should be contrasted, such as *a* and *d*, *c* and *o*, *m* and *n*, so that the child can see differences and gain some form of reference other than having to rely solely upon rote memory, which would be the case where letters were learned separately.

Hence we can establish the need for matching and contrasting activities of short duration in which the *child* carries out the activity. Seeing the letters is not enough; the comparison and matching of the letters must be done by the child, and one obvious way of doing this is by using letters, cut from plywood, in a variety of matching and sorting activities. For example, when shown a word, the children must pick out matching wooden letters; where letters are repeated in a word or sentence, they should be noted; where a wooden letter has been wrongly chosen, the correct and the incorrect letters are compared; and a variety of idiosyncratic activities should be used such as picking out all the 'tall' letters, all the rounded letters, and so on. In these activities the words with which the letters are matched should always stand in a sentence in order to retain the idea of letters as part of written language, even though the activities begin when the child enters school and before any attempt is made to teach the sounds of letters. Gradually, this type of activity will evolve into one in which sound begins to play a prominent part.

As the child begins to obtain a clearer notion of the composition of written language and to learn a little about words and letters, he will be passing imperceptibly from a predominantly intuitive form of thinking to what Piaget has called concrete operational thought. His thinking no longer dwells unduly upon his immediate actions and he is able to think outside his present environment. Additionally, he is able to develop powers of analysis and to consider the whole in terms of its parts, an activity essential in word discrimination and identification (Goins, 1958). But it is a critical period, and one that should not be rushed by the teacher, otherwise cognitive confusion will surely result. Throughout the whole period covered in learning to read, the danger is that the child may be asked to do things that are beyond his cognitive powers or that he does not fully understand. (By 'understand', of course, it is not meant that he will be able to explain what he is doing, but rather that he will be able to use the knowledge he has, and the strategies that he has developed, in order to complete the task.)

There are six main stages of instruction in the approach to teaching reading that I advocate in this chapter. Perhaps the most problematic stage is that at which the child is given his first reading book. At that point the child has completed the first stage of instruction and moves according to almost universal practice from a preparatory language-experience approach to a word and phrase identification approach based on a set text. In order to cope with this, the child has to rely heavily upon his memory of words and of letter sounds; he must try as best he can to exercise his powers of phonic analysis and synthesis in order to produce the sounds occasioned by the print; and all this has to be done at the time when the child is least competent to exercise these skills. He may have a store of words that he can recognize at sight, but the effort of recalling them may be so distracting that all meaning is lost (and there is little enough meaning in the first books of most published reading schemes!) Thus the young reader's first encounter with a 'real' book, to be read by himself, often turns out to be a meaningless experience in terms of the message received. What pleasure he gets turns upon the mechanical activity of word calling, and the whole approach is based upon the general assumption that the reader relies primarily upon the use of phonological cues and the summation of sounds — an assumption that cannot stand up to scrutiny, as demonstrated at the beginning of this chapter.

What is needed at the second stage is not a test of memory for words, which is unpredictable, nor a test of phonic skills which the child does not have, but a programme that allows him to use those skills in language he has developed, and to associate those skills with others he has still to acquire.

The child between the ages of five and six years, although his spoken language is not fully developed (Crystal, 1976) is nevertheless reasonably competent in its use. Furthermore, he will have been introduced to some aspects of the correspondence between spoken and written language if the *Breakthrough* type of materials have been used as mentioned above. Hence, we should look for some means of continuing the sequence begun in the earlier stage, namely, of going from the known to the unknown and of avoiding the need for detailed analysis before the reading activity takes place.

The obvious answer seems to be to use as texts stories that are known orally, or can be easily learned, by the children. The reading of the texts would then result in the child's recalling the stories, a task which would be much easier and more pleasurable than recalling the sounds to be attached to letters and words; and against these recalled stories, he would match the written presentation. Nursery rhymes and folk tales are an obvious source of such stories, and so are many of the jingles that children chant (Opie and Opie, 1951, 1969). They are widely known and memorable, and have demonstrated their durability in that they have interested many generations of children, who do not seem to tire of repeating them. If children were asked to repeat these rhymes and stories — which they willingly do at home and in the playground — while looking at the text, they would gradually begin to associate particular written forms with words as spoken, and the reading activity would be to locate the symbolic forms of some of the things said.

Having learned to locate, and thereby to identify in a personal way, certain words, phrases and sentences, the third stage is to require the child to use these symbolic forms. The activity changes from that of matching print to speech to the composition of a text where the composer is constrained in his use of words more or less to those used in the nursery rhyme or folk story with which he has just been dealing. This resumption of the *Breakthrough* technique is similar in nature to the first stage, but it differs in its objective. No longer are the child's actions and accompanying speech the basis for the composition. Now he is expected to use the words of the texts, adding his own words only in order to supplement those from the texts. This will complete a two-way process: receiving the words at stage two and supplying or using the words constructively at stage three. In practical terms, it will mean that the teacher has to add to the teacher's sentence maker (*Breakthrough to Literacy*) words taken from the nursery rhymes and folk tales for use in this group activity.

The forms of organization used at these first three stages will vary. At stage 1, the activities will be mainly group activities led by the teacher, but for children who make rapid progress there may be some movement towards the use of individual sentence makers. At stage 2, there will be reading together within the group, individual reading within the group, and in some cases isolated reading by children. At stage 3, all the discussion and much of the composition will be on a group basis.

The reason for this strong emphasis on group teaching is two-fold:

it avoids the isolation of the learner when engaged in tasks where he is operating to the limits of his ability, and it ensures a firm control of what is taught. It also means that children who are at approximately the same level of ability face tasks together, with the possibility of increased understanding through seeing how others accomplish a task.

Stage 4 will form a bridge between what the child has learned from his reading activities thus far and what he will need to learn in order to read books at a later stage. It will be a stage which will be gradually introduced and interwoven with stage 3 and will involve a closer examination of language — sentences, phrases and words — used in the first three stages, as well as the comparison of this language with similar forms taken from literature which will be read at stages 5 and 6. (This would be the beginning of the activity formerly known as the development of word attack skills.) The child should be encouraged to look for comparisons in the form of texts: sentences that contain similar phrases, words with similarities in structure, sound sequences that correspond, and for meanings expressed similarly or differently. Phrases such as *on the, in the; there is, there was* can be extracted, and words can be compared: *cat* with *hat* or *can, shop* with *ship* or *shot, hear* with *heard, here* with *there*. These exercises will lead to the identification of letter strings: blends, digraphs — which are meaningless alone (*ea* differs in *idea, bear, bean* and so on) — within consonant settings; syllables that form the basic units of pronunciation; and the spelling patterns, which form the critical units for the purposes of word identification (Gibson 1970). Ultimately, however, it is from the morphemic units of words that meaning is derived (see Chomsky, 1970), and hence the importance of allowing children to make comparisons between words such as *hear* and *heard, cycle* and *bicycle*, where similarity in morphemic structure is emphasized.

The more readily available means of reproducing material in schools (such as Banda machines) enable the teacher to provide copies of texts which can be cut up and then reconstructed to match the master copy, and the words can be bent to display the pronounceable parts of the word and to emphasize word structure.

At the 5th stage, group and individual work will continue, and the activities will now turn to what is more traditionally thought of as reading activity in school. The children will be provided with texts constructed from the words used in stages 2 to 4. Obviously, this will be quite a task for the teacher in the first place, but the benefits to the children will be tremendous. Instead of being faced with books from the normal reading scheme, which, because of control and limitations of vocabulary present a form of written English emaciated almost beyond recognition, the child will be able to enjoy a wide vocabulary, all of which is to some extent familiar. The texts may not have the style of accomplished authors, but they could scarcely be poorer than the normal fare provided, especially in the early books of basic reading schemes, and they would be relevant to the child's previous learning experiences.

At stage 6 published texts by authors of some substance would be introduced. The children will have been prepared for this at stages 4 and 5, where they will have met examples of the language structure of these books and many of the commonly used phrases, and will have studied a substantial number of the words used in the books. Basic reading schemes, eliminating early inane books, could be used, and so could non-fiction books such as the Macdonald Information Series. The latter would cater for those children with a liking for factual knowledge, who are not so interested in imaginative stories.

These stages are sequential, but they need not, and in fact probably should not, be exclusive. The difference between these proposals and the old look-and-say approach is that they are language-based rather than word-based. They are also activity-based rather than primarily sight-based, and the stages are fully integrated, each stage being specifically preparatory to the subsequent stages.

To ensure success, each teacher would need to spend about three days preparing a programme based on these stages. For stage 2, many duplicated copies of nursery rhymes, jingles and folk stories (copied from the *Faber Book of Folk Tales* rather than from 'simplified' adaptations) would be needed. Some of these copies could be cut up into segments — sentences, phrases, words — to be used at stages 3 and 4. For stage 5, simple stories, restricted closely to the words and phrases used in those rhymes and tales, could be constructed. For stage 6, the teacher will have to decide upon the texts to be used, and from them extract and make copies of sentences, phrases and words on separate pieces of card, which can be used at stages 4 and 5 for comparison with the words encountered in the original material for those stages. In this way, the child will be prepared at each stage for the ensuing stages. The whole scheme will be integrated and sequential. Learning will proceed from the known and the concrete to the abstract, in that all the stories will be known at stage 2; and where the story is not known (stages 5 and 6), the lexical content (words) and to some extent the syntactic elements (in the limited form of phrases) will be familiar. Hence the child will be encountering texts in which at least one, if not more, of the three aspects of language — the lexical, syntactic and the semantic — will be familiar. He is not faced, as so often happens when traditional approaches are used, with an entirely new text, where he does not know the story, where the phraseology is unfamiliar, and when it is merely hoped that his previous experience will have ensured that he remembers a sufficient number of the words, which he can recognize reasonably quickly, in order to maintain a sufficient momentum of reading to be able to grasp the meaning.

It is argued in this chapter, as the findings of Burke (1976) seem to suggest, that teachers have too readily accepted that ability in word identification is synonymous with ability to comprehend a text fully, and that the answer would surely lie not in pushing the child more closely to identify words, but in changing the system in order to develop the use of semantic and syntactic cues right from the early stages. Word spotting has too easily been accepted in place of language interpretation, and language interpretation is what reading is all about at every point in a child's progress. Furthermore, we do not always pay sufficient attention to the necessity for prior knowledge in any reading exercise, a point to which we should have been alerted by Ausubel's (1968) theory concerning the benefits of advance organizers — advance information that prepares the learner for the ensuing task.

Finally, having outlined an approach to suit the learner and the task, it is essential that we provide a form of organization that will ensure optimum learning. A constant source of danger throughout the entire period when children are learning to read is that they may become passive in their reactions to texts, and this can most easily occur when the reader is reading alone, either silently or aloud.

Earlier in this chapter, reference was made to the dangers of the isolation of the learner. This has certainly happened with many of the activities connected with the teaching of reading at all levels. The teacher who merely listens to children read and helps them to sound out the occasional word is allowing the child to operate mainly in isolation.

Unless she requires the child to work out a possible meaning in order to derive the desired response to the unknown word, and unless she requires the child to re-tell the story at frequent intervals, she cannot be sure that the reader is reacting fully to the task.

A similar situation occurs in many schools when children are 'doing comprehension exercises' or projects. They work at the texts alone, and they provide answers that are accepted as right or wrong, and there the matter rests. There is little discussion with the child about his reaction; there is little attempt to ensure that he sees how others have reacted under similar circumstances; and in some cases the teacher does not bother to ensure that the reader knows how to set about reacting to the particular text.

One way to break this isolation and ensure adequate training is to rely more heavily than has been the normal practice upon group work, where the emphasis should be on the interactions within the group about the text. Much group work in the past left the participants virtually isolated, because only answers, rather than reactions to answers, were required. At the literal level there is frequently little to react to or to become involved with: the answer is straightforward and it is a simple matter of re-checking if it is wrong. It is, however, a different matter when inferences are being drawn. Here the reader must go beyond the printed text and deploy arguments to make a case. It is much more difficult to correct a reader who has made a mistaken inference, unless the teacher or a successful reader is prepared to demonstrate how the text was used and express the arguments which were deployed. If this is done, then the student who made the mistake will begin to realize what strategies he should have used.

The duplicating machine and the overhead projector have made group work of this type a much more viable proposition. Small groups can be brought together for a short session in which the teacher and all the members of the group discuss the text in detail. A range of texts can easily be built up, stored, and used repeatedly with different groups of children. Short extracts from good literature provide unlimited scope for this type of work.

The value of learning to construct a written text as part of children's introduction to learning to read applies equally to the development of reading skills. The written work of children should be scrutinized by others, and group reactions should provide the basis for a review of the work by the writer. This allows the child to compare the message he wishes to convey with the way in which it is received and written — a useful insight into the possible variations in the deep and surface structures of written language.

Another way of helping the reader react to a text is through the use of *cloze procedure* (Taylor, 1957), in which certain words are omitted from the text and the reader is expected to replace them. Again, in individual work there is the possibility of isolating the reader, so that his answer is given and simply marked right or wrong, without any opportunity for him to learn how he should have approached the tasks. Co-operative group action would reduce this possibility and suggest a variety of strategies used by other readers.

One point worth stressing about the use of cloze procedure is that the extraction of every 'n'th word will not normally give the teacher sufficient control over the requirements in each exercise. The controlled extraction of specific types of words, or words in a specific setting, would provide the opportunity for the teacher to prepare and control the activities of the group, and would enable the reader to develop and practise particular techniques such as reading ahead, comparing two or more statements in order to derive another inference, or cross-checking semantic, syntactic and phonological cues. Such exercises would involve a substantial amount of preparation by the teacher, but the rewards could be considerable, provided the exercise were made into an engrossing group activity in which the children reacted to the texts and through them to one another.

The justifications for the arguments presented in this paper have been based mainly upon the demands of the learner and the task. There is, however, a further consideration that concerns the teachers. While the suggested approach would involve more work for teachers, both in terms of preparation and of a more active participation in the teaching process, it would also provide them with a cohesive and integrated plan of action in which the objectives are perfectly clear.

The latter point is particularly important for newly-trained teachers. Many of the older text books on the teaching of reading dwell heavily upon the possibilities of confusion facing children who are learning to read, and it is difficult for the teacher to see a way through the difficulties and to determine what to do about them. In fact, the points where confusion can arise are multitudinous and very difficult to detect in many instances. All that the inexperienced teacher can hope to do is to attempt to clarify for children the main processes involved in reading, such as the consideration of words and letters in their context, and blending and searching behaviour as a reaction to a text. The emphasis should be on action in certain easily determined situations, rather than on the diagnosis of specific and sometimes detailed difficulties. Thus the teacher can be regarded as the general practitioner that he or she usually is, and not the clinician who could not hope to deal with thirty children in the same way as with one child in a clinic. The approach that is proposed in this chapter provides the framework; it also provides scope for the experienced teacher to develop in the children an understanding and appreciation of written language at all levels.

References

Ausubel, D. P. (1968) *Educational Psychology: A Cognitive View.* New York: Holt, Rinehart and Winston.

Bartlett, F. C. (1947) 'The measurement of human skill,' *British Medical Journal, 4510,* 835–8 and *4511,* 877–80.

Burke, E. (1976) 'A developmental study of children's reading strategies,' *Educational Review, 29,* 30–48.

Chomsky, C. (1970) 'Reading, writing and phonology,' *Harvard Educational Review, 40,* 287–309.

Crystal, D. (1976) *Child Language, Learning and Linguistics.* London: Arnold.

Des (1975) *A Language for Life* (The Bullock Report). London: HMSO.

Downing, J. (1972) 'Children's developing concepts of spoken and written language,' *Journal of Reading Behaviour, 4,* 1–19.

Gibson, E. J. (1965) 'Learning to read,' *Science, 148,* 1066–72.

Gibson, E. J., Schurcliff, A. and Yonas, A. (1970) 'Utilization of spelling patterns by deaf and hearing subjects,' in Levin, H. and Williams, J. P. Eds. *Basic Studies on Reading,* New York: Basic Books.

Goins, J. T. (1958) 'Visual perceptual abilities and early reading progress,' *Supplementary Educational Monographs, No. 87.*

Goodman, K. S. (1973) *The Psycholinguistic Nature of the Reading Process.* Detroit: Wayne State University Press.

Huey, E. B. (1908) *The Psychology and Pedagogy of Reading.* New York: Macmillan (reprinted in 1973 by the MIT Press).

Mackay, D., Thompson, B. and Schaub, P. (1970) *Breakthrough to Literacy.* London: Longman.

Opie, I. and Opie, P. (1951) *The Oxford Dictionary of Nursery Rhymes.* Oxford: Clarendon.

Opie, I. and Opie, P. (1969) *The Lore and Language of School Children*. London: Oxford University Press.

Pick, A. D. (1965) 'Improvement of visual and tactual form discrimination,' *Journal of Experimental Psychology, 69*, 331–9.

Reid, J. F. (1966) 'Learning to think about reading,' *Educational Research, 9*, 56–62.

Roberts, T. (1975) 'Skills of analysis and synthesis in the early stages of reading,' *British Journal of Educational Psychology, 45*, 3–9.

Roberts, T. (1977) 'The language of children and their reading books,' *Education, 3—13, 6*, 37–9.

Smith, F. (1971) *Understanding Reading*. New York: Holt, Rinehart and Winston.

Taylor, W. L. (1957) 'Close readability scores as indices of individual differences in comprehension and aptitude,' *Journal of Applied Psychology, 41*, 19–26.

Thorndike, E. L. (1917) 'Reading as reasoning: a study of mistakes in paragraph reading,' *Journal of Educational Psychology*, 8, 323–32.

Vygotsky, L. S. (1962) *Thought and Language*. Cambridge, Mass.: The MIT Press.

4

English
in the
Later Primary Years

ELIZABETH and DAVID GRUGEON

The 1944 White Paper 'Educational Reconstruction' reminds us of major constraints on British junior schools at the time. English was by no means free of these constraints:

> Instead of the junior schools performing their proper and highly important function of fostering the potentialities of children at an age when their minds are nimble and receptive, their curiosity strong, their imagination fertile and their spirits high, the curriculum is too often cramped and distorted by over-emphasis on examination subjects and on ways and means of defeating the examiners. The blame for this rests not with the teachers but with the system.

However, thirty years later, with the pressures of selective examinations at eleven lifted in so many parts of the country, Bullock (DES, 1975) was to report:

> In our visits to schools we found that the teaching of language through weekly exercises was still commonly to be found at all age levels, but particularly in the primary school. . . . In the main such work was not a reinforcement of something newly learned in the course of some other classroom activity, but a task performed outside any context which would give it meaning.

The curriculum still remains 'cramped and distorted' and nowhere more so than in language work. There is a sad modesty about the word 'suggesting' in the following sentence from Bullock:

> What we are suggesting, then, is that children should learn about language by experiencing it and experimenting with its use.

If Bullock is right, much that passes for 'English' in the junior school is largely irrelevant to language development. While we could speculate on the reasons why teachers continue to resort to exercises with gobbets of language in textbooks for children at this age (ease of control, support from parents, false language theories and so on) it may be more fruitful to explore the positive side of English teaching and language development — in the upper stages of primary schools at their best. The rest of this chapter looks at some concrete examples and some of the theoretical studies that exemplify the following propositions emerging from good practice:

(a) learning is personal and co-operative;
(b) English, being the language we speak, write and read, permeates the whole curriculum;
(c) literature has a vital part to play in personal and curriculum development;
(d) the school is a limited language environment which can be enlarged;
(e) language can be developed if the child's world is brought into the classroom;
(f) while some models can constrict, a strong and diverse experience of stories and poems can enhance children's power to write.

Consider Peter, ten years old and in his final year at an inner London primary school; he had a reading age of 9.9 on the Schonell scale, a lively personality like most of his group, and went to school in a rather run-down nineteenth century building in a very run-down inner urban area. At the start of his last year of primary education he was not reading or writing a great deal, but by the end of that year he had become enthusiastic about both. During the summer term his records showed that he had read eighteen fiction books and his folder of work contained two books of his own writing including up to thirty poems. He was confident about choosing books to read and independent in choosing subjects to write about. This was a fairly typical result of the work of a team of teachers who were responsible for the ninety or so nine- to eleven-year-olds. Their programme of integrated work involved joint decisions about the topics to be covered and the devolution of responsibility for guiding these topics to teachers who felt most confident in a particular curriculum area. Responsibility for reading development was taken by all, but in different ways; at the two extremes one teacher dealt with a small remedial retrieval group for intensive repair work while another took a large group of confident readers whom she monitored carefully into further confidence in reading fiction for pleasure.

Poetry and drama grew out of topics and in their turn stimulated topics for further development. In Peter's case the base group in which he spent most of his time was an environment that very much encouraged encounters with poetry. A range of poetry anthologies was available in the book corner (never more than four copies of an anthology, only one copy of the more expensive, to offer maximum variety). There was also a box of single poems mounted on cards, so that children could pick a poem at random. The teacher cut these out of magazines and old BBC school publications, or copied them from selections not available in school, and mounted them with accompanying pictures, secured by a transparent cover to firm pieces of card. The rationale for this was a belief that children with even slight reading problems are deterred by anthologies where they must search for a poem among many others. She felt that individual cards with related pictures to attract the child's attention would induce many more children to attempt to read poems. This proved to be true. Children selected poems in passing, groups took one each and read to each other; others asked to copy out and mount poems and add pictures — their own drawings or something found in the class box of pictures from magazines — or even to turn their own poems into cards that could contribute to a growing group collection of poems.

Why poems? As classrooms offer children experiences of objects from the outside world to handle, talk and think about, so a box or book of poems gives them an opportunity to think about someone else's thoughts, to discover new perspectives, and to experience the power of words to convey an individual's ideas and feelings about his world. It was in an environment where poems were read a great deal and talked about in a very relaxed way that Peter and the rest of his class began to discover that they enjoyed writing poems — or small pieces of prose in a precise and carefully structured way — for themselves.

For many of them the writing demanded by teachers was not an end in itself. Peter and his friends were engaged for almost a month in building a working model of a lighthouse. It occupied them almost all the time and involved a lot of reference to books for the practical information required — not only the measurements and structure of a lighthouse but the complexities of wiring it. They shopped for the necessary items to have not only a light but a buzzer for a foghorn. All the time they talked; they drew and measured and made rough notes for working purposes. When at last the three-foot model was winking and buzzing from its convincing rocky island (just like the one they'd seen on a school journey) the piece of writing to describe what they had just done seemed very flat and thin. The activity, the process of making, of working in a group, the frustrations and the satisfactions were not something they could either recall or adequately record. 'Peter, Brian, Kevin and John made a model of the lighthouse' was no reflection of the way it had really been. Yet this was not something that *needed* writing about. Language had been strongly developed by their planning, negotiating, reading, speculating and discussing. Neither the writing nor the information now possessed about lighthouses and their construction was the goal or benefit of the activity.

There *are* times when writing becomes the principal activity, and frequently that year it happened with the writing of poems. Peter wrote in his rough book, entirely off his own bat:

A Paper	*The Wind*
Lots of words	The wind
Exciting things to read	blows strongly,
Football results	Something soft
Then you throw	The wind is invisible
It away	No Colour
	Just blows.

This was an entirely self-sufficient activity involving the making of a thoughtful and unique observation — structuring an idea, catching it before it got away. In a way this seemed to be what poetry had to offer — ways of looking at things for yourself and shaping ideas. The models for this kind of writing can only be a diversity of other poems — adults' and children's. A child should not have a static idea of what a poem is, but a sense of the infinite possibilities and flexibility of language, and, most important of all, an awareness of the flexibility and variety of his own language. It is likely that a BBC *Living Language* broadcast some weeks previously had provided Peter with a model for these two poems. The programme had included a number of Japanese haiku. The class teacher had not asked the children to write their own but had read the broadcast poems many times again and added some of them to the poem box so that the children could become familiar with them. Poems are infinitely re-readable and the ones children enjoy become very much part of the way they write. A West Indian girl became so intoxicated by Tennyson's *Eagle* that she actually produced the poem, copied in her own handwriting: 'He clasps the crag with crooked hands', convinced that she had written it herself! And that is how it should be! (At this point, it might be useful to look back at our initial propositions, starting with 'learning is personal and co-operative,' and see how far they have already been exemplified in the description of work in Peter's school.)

Literature and the curriculum

If English, as our shared language, permeates the whole curriculum, what of the role of literature? It is worth considering what it is that literature has to offer in other areas of the curriculum and, in return, what experiences in other subjects may bring to the reading of a novel or a selection of poems. Stories and poems are very often drawn upon during the course of work in other curriculum areas. It is often easier for primary and middle school teachers to find literature that relates directly to their work in science, nature study, or history and to draw it into all kinds of projects. (The Bullock Report suggests positive ways in which schools might implement a book policy to help teachers assemble a range of fiction and non-fiction books in response to both planned and spontaneous needs.) Do the children who construct their own kite in the classroom and take it out for a test flight on the school field bring something more to a story like Bill Naughton's about the kite (1957)? Perhaps they feel like the boys in the story as they struggle to fly their kite, share their exhilaration and understand the sense of overwhelming loss as the kite pulls free:

> The string went over the house and disappeared. It'll be falling, falling,
> falling, far, far away. Falling like a great broken bird, far from the
> street. Herbert's face was strained and grey.
>
> "Well, that's the last I'll ever see o' that, Michael."
>
> "Eee, I'm sorry Herbert," he said, "I saw it come up an' I shouted."

We can only hypothesize that they may make more of this story, or
that the story may reinforce elements of their own recent experience
and give it another dimension. They have learned something about
aero-dynamics, air currents, the structure of surfaces and balance;
they have experienced working in a group using wood and
polystyrene; they have shared decisions and made practical
judgments. They have also shared in the emotional experience of
success and the pleasure of seeing the thing they have made
operating as they had hoped it would. The story may remind them
of the way they felt and sharpen their understanding. And at the
same time they may read or listen to the story itself with greater
interest and insight.

Finding the right story or poem is sometimes a problem when a
teacher is looking for specific relevance. That is when a school needs
a teacher or librarian whose job is to advise colleagues on the range
of alternatives and help them to arrive at a book policy. A teacher
working on a project in history may have no idea about the
availability or suitability of a number of historical novels, and yet to
ignore this resource would be a great pity. As Anna Davin (1976)
writes:

> The personalizing of history is the potential strength of the historical
> novel, enabling it to impart a richer historical understanding than
> formal history books can usually give.

Apart from bringing history alive, historical novels act as models for
children's own writing, helping them to see ways in which history
can be about people and particularly about children. Alongside the
facts, they can produce imaginative reconstructions in writing and
in drama of what it must have been like to live in another age.

A teacher who is doing work on spiders may be glad to be
introduced to E. B. White's *Charlotte's Web* (1963), while work on

animal intelligence may be enriched by a reading of Robert O'Brien's *Mrs. Frisby and the Rats of NIMH* (1973). Conversely, children who have read these books may be stimulated to begin a study of spiders and/or to consider ways of testing the intelligence of the class guinea pig or gerbil.

All this is not to suggest that poems and stories should be introduced only as 'related material', to be used in conjunction with other work, either as a starting point or to add another dimension. Stories and poems need to be encountered head on for what they are.

Bringing the child's world in

What is it that is unique and valuable about a child's encounter with stories and poems? Probably the fact that it is chiefly through literature, and quite particularly through poetry, that the reader comes up against another individual's feelings conveyed through a particular verbal form. Children's feelings are bursting out all the time, and too often little of the excitement and novelty of their lives comes back at them in any shape or form. Schools are institutions where their experience is ordered, but rarely in an affective way. Feeling is subdued, the irrational is shaped into the rational and the excitement of discovery is tamed by explanation.

It is often only in drama, literature and art that encounters with emotion are legitimate and actively encouraged and the child's 'feeling' life is positively nurtured. The models we offer them for writing, drama and art compete with the powerful models of television programmes. Much of what they are currently watching on television affects their talk and their imaginative play and drama, and emerges in their written work. The images of cartoons, commercials and light comedy pervade their behaviour and their thinking. A group of children wrote a book together. The hero is a monster:

> The name of our monster is called Henry. He has big pointed teeth down to his chin, and he has a big tail. When he gets out of bed (which he never does). But when he does he is in a very bad temper and he always throws his plates about. He has got gigantic ears and a bump on his head. He has got a purple jumper and striped trousers. He is a cross-eyed monster and always falling over a lot of things. He has got a little bit of hair on his head and whiskers on his nose. He has got skelington like hands and feet and has a point on the end of his tail.

It is easy to see Henry's origins in comics and television and in the children's own view of the world. Henry's adventures are pure slapstick — he frightens old ladies, plays hide and seek with animals in the zoo, makes himself ill eating sweets, turns on firehoses, drops school dinners, sits on the headmaster's lap by accident ('The headmaster went red as a cherry'), and is finally disposed of after an application of the cane! It seems superficial, and yet for the group of girls involved it was a serious and very careful piece of work. Beneath its apparent triviality there is a concern for real events in their everyday lives: Henry goes to bed early with a cup of cocoa when he feels miserable, makes careful shopping lists, cleans his teeth, and generally behaves like the average ten year old girl. The models in this case are powerful but the children's real experience seems to accommodate and override them.

It is useless to ignore the Bionic Woman or the Wombles; the problem is to find ways of helping children to cope with formula humour and stereotyped situations. The situation is not entirely new, although today's out-of-school literary models may be more powerful than they once were. But most English teachers are part of the tradition that it is important to get the child's world into the classroom. This aim was described as a 'preoccupation' by Jeremy Mulford in a classic chapter in 'Directions in the Teaching of English' (Thompson, 1969). He lists a succession of influential books on English teaching written in the previous fifteen years: *Free Writing* (1956), by Dora Pym; *Coming into Their Own* (1959), by Marjorie Hourd and G. E. Cooper; *Young Writers, Young Readers* (1960), edited by Boris Ford; *Let the Children Write* (1961), by Margaret Langdon; *English for Maturity* (1961) and *English for the Rejected* (1964), by David Holbrook; *English in Education* (1962), edited by Brian Jackson and Denys Thompson; *An Experiment in Education* (1963), by Sybil Marshall; and *The Excitement of Writing* (1964), edited by A. B. Clegg.

In 1960 James Britton challenged,

> Let us stop worrying about the child's lack of ideas, lack of experience, poor environment, and concentrate upon his ability to deal with what experience he has. (Ford, *Young Writers, Young Readers.*)

For many of us looking towards the 1980s this is still central to the way we think. The pervasiveness of television culture is now part of the children's experience, which we must draw in and draw upon. The fact that a child watches so many hours of television a week does not preclude the possibility that private reading may offer a significant experience at the same time.

Take as an example Betsy Byars's book, *The Eighteenth Emergency* (1976). It is about two days in the life of a small boy who is frightened of the school bully; he comes to terms with his fear by deliberately confronting the bigger boy. Within this simple framework, Byars writes a wonderfully sympathetic and humourous study of children's loneliness in an adult world, of the sheer enormity of imagined fear that a child can carry with him, of the gulf between children and their parents, of the sustaining nature of childhood friendship and of the vital role that fantasy plays in helping children to deal with the reality of their own lives. Benjie, or Mouse as he is to his friends, longs for a father who stays at home instead of driving long distance lorries, and a mother less preoccupied with her work. He envies the apparently more secure and supportive families of his friends and during the course of the book is seen growing in understanding of himself, of the bully as a person, of his mother and of the strange old man next door. Many strands are woven in a story that is both complex in the issues it deals with and yet accessible to its child audience.

Not all children's books mirror life as sensitively as this one does, but when they do they can be a source of reassurance and personal insight. A most important criterion for the choice of books, plays and poems may be their relevance to the lives and present stage of development of the children who encounter them. Books need to be selected not only for a curriculum area but for relevance to the individual child's emotional and intellectual needs. Books can extend the child's experience and are, as Frank Whitehead writes, (in Thompson, 1969) 'a supremely potent mode of significant experience.'

Developing independence in reading

The teacher of an upper junior class is responsible for selecting a range of novels suitable for the range of individual development that any group of children will present. Reading aloud to a whole group remains an important activity, but the careful monitoring of individual reading becomes vital. Bullock stresses this:

> There is no doubt at all in our mind that one of the most important tasks facing the teacher of older juniors and younger secondary pupils is to increase the amount and the range of their voluntary reading.

The report draws attention to the tendency for schools to take away the props once a child has mastered the decoding process involved in learning to read, leaving children to find suitable fiction for themselves. Many children, left on their own once they have completed graded readers, give up reading fiction almost as soon as they are ready for it, simply because they don't know what to choose:

> We noticed that this was related to the teacher's discontinuance of any kind of record of the child's reading. As long as the child was engaged on the reading scheme or the graded readers supplementary to it, the teacher would usually keep a note of his progress through it. But we met few teachers who kept records of what the child read after this.

Why should there be such an emphasis on the availability of fiction and the monitoring of individual voluntary reading, apart from our concern for children's personal development? The Bullock report refers to Frank Whitehead's (1975) Schools Council Survey of Children's Reading Interests and concludes that 'it was clear that the narrative mode provided for children of all ages by far the strongest motivation towards the reading of books.' They note, however, that 'narrative books are substantially outnumbered by non-fiction in most primary schools.' Perhaps this is partly due to the emphasis on a wide range of reference books of information to support immediate ongoing needs. In a junior school where teachers are involved in bold curriculum experiments incorporating group work, integration of various subjects and the sharing of learning experiences through talk, there may be little time for children to do quiet individual reading with adequate adult help. Thus it was encouraging to read the uncompromising tone of Bullock:

> Every primary school classroom should therefore have a book corner, partly enclosed and occupying the quitest area of the room.

The availability of a range of suitable fiction (changed over the weeks) in every classroom depends on the collective knowledge of the teachers, librarians and advisers of what is available. In the last twenty years the growth in children's literature has been enormous. For a class teacher to supply and monitor each child's private reading of good imaginative literature is a daunting job: but within each class, the teacher has to face the task of developing self-initiated reading. This can be achieved most simply by keeping a record of each child's reading and by paying particular attention to children when they are choosing a new book. A child who has enjoyed reading a book is often disappointed by finishing it and can react by not wanting to try another. Again, Bullock suggests a number of imaginative and practical ways of dealing with the problem of individual progress in reading.

Ten years ago the suggestion that teachers might 'tape trailer passages on cassettes for children to listen to on headsets' might have seemed far-fetched. Technology, in the form of tape recorders, ciné-cameras, instamatics and sophisticated reprographic equipment, has broadened the scope of English teaching. Now drama and movement can be extended by the use of sound effects taped in music lessons or turned into film or even video-tape. Written work can be printed and illustrated in book form to very high standards by the children themselves or at local teachers' centres. The exchange of writing (stories, letters, autobiography and poetry) between classes within schools and between schools has raised the status and purpose of the function of writing by making it possible for children to write for an audience beyond their own teacher and their own classmates.

Writing and the influence of models

The narrative styles and forms of stories are probably as important to children's language development as the content of stories may be to their personal development. The potent story model (growing from gossip, television and, for some, story books at home, into regular stories at school) provides a successful and sustaining form for much dramatic play and for writing. Probably the best writing that most upper primary school children do is in story form. The abundant opportunity, over many years, to gain a confident and secure mastery of a constructed narrative shape seems to enable the development of advanced skills of hypothesizing, speculation and the consideration of alternative possibilities.

It is not really surprising, for much learning theory emphasizes the need to make sense of new ideas and new knowledge by relating them to our existing ideas, 'making the unfamiliar familiar' as James Britton (1970) puts it. And if Bullock is right to emphasize how much we learn by *talking* about new experience, then the kind of writing that is closest to the way we talk is likely to be the soundest preparation for other kinds of writing in the long term. Narratives require narrators — the words suggest their origins in an oral culture which is still very much the culture of early schooldays. Narrative writing — diary, direct recording of observed experience, and imaginative story — can be a seedbed for more diverse kinds of writing later on.

In the secondary school, the curriculum will demand various kinds of notes, summaries, reports, descriptions, analyses, tests, examinations, essays, stories, poems and plays. The Writing Research Unit at London University Institute of Education, after studying thousands of pieces of writing collected from secondary schools, came up with two main sets of propositions regarding the various functions of writing and the various audiences for writing (Martin *et al.*, 1976). Broadly speaking, the study suggests that there are three general language functions that can be defined, and that in every piece of writing one of these three functions predominates. The three functions are *transactional, expressive* and *poetic*. Adopting the guidelines from the briefing document used by the researchers attached to the unit, we can say that:

> *transactional* writing is concerned with an end outside itself. It is concerned to satisfy the reader who is seeking information: it informs, persuades, instructs;

> *expressive* writing seems to satisfy the writer's desire to verbalize his thoughts and feelings – either to himself or to someone who is willing to be interested in them and him;

> *poetic* writing seems to exist for its own sake and to be a deliberately shaped verbal construct made for the pleasure of making it and sharing it.

Young children's most successful writing is mostly expressive; it is the way in which immediate impressions are most naturally recorded and conveyed in a friendly, informal manner. This is sometimes seen as lazy or slipshod by the adult purveyor of knowledge who has mastered the particular conventions that traditionally accompany some disciplines at higher levels — for example, that certain information should only be offered in the third person or the past tense. Research into the development of writing at primary level is pretty sparse, but it appears likely that *imposed* forms of transactional writing limit children's access to their own thinking and language resources. Children's early writing can develop by age eleven into a very wide range of individual styles and 'voices'. The style, form and shape for their writing, determined only partly at a conscious level, is an inseparable element of their thinking. In early transactional writing, then, we should welcome a strongly expressive tone, which suggests 'personal' thinking rather than 'correct' thinking.

However, there are distinct complications with adopting too simple a *credo* that might say, for example, that practice and increased competence in expressive writing will naturally help children to master transactional writing, which involves more impersonal and abstract forms of language.

Nancy Martin, herself a researcher for the Writing Research Unit, reported on her study of a week's output in writing from three classes, one of children aged seven, one of eleven-year-olds, and one of nine-year-olds (in Jones and Mulford, 1971). At age seven it seemed that more complex language occurred in the children's stories than in other kinds of writing, but it was more difficult to generalize about the eleven-year-olds' writing. For some older children, certain story models were restricting, and their transactional writing was more developed. Yet, though a fair number of children showed conceptual thinking and generalization in their transactional writing, the majority still showed in this type of writing

a scatter of disassociated ideas, whereas their stories are structured by narrative form, by their feelings and by their own experience. So for most children stories (and poems) are the means by which they use language most effectively and comprehensively.

Theory into practice — or practice into theory — or both?

The best work in English from children aged seven to thirteen, in our view, has come as a result of a confident interaction between practitioners and theorists — or even a merger of the two. Teachers and researchers have developed a shared language for talking about children's writing, children's talking and teachers' talking. Teachers' centres at their best have become theory and practice workshops for the exchange of experience and the testing out of ideas.

Think of the Schools Council/NATE *Children as Readers* (1975) project, with local groups of teachers in England and Wales making tapes and transcripts of groups of children discussing poems and short stories; the co-operative analysis of thousands of samples of children's writing in the *Writing Across the Curriculum* project (Martin, *et al.*, 1976) and the examples studied and presented by Connie and Harold Rosen (1973).

We know much more now about why we value the child's own language and experience, about why we foster it in art, music, drama, movement, talk and writing, about the reasons for structuring classrooms and schools for maximum co-operative small group working. We are starting to involve the parents, grandparents and the community to enrich the linguistic and cultural resources of a school system unlikely to be able to expand its work force of paid professional staff.

References

Britton, J. N. (1970) *Language and Learning.* Harmondsworth: Allen Lane, The Penguin Press.

Byars, B. (1976) *The Eighteenth Emergency* (Puffin). Harmondsworth: Penguin Books.

Davin, A. (1976) 'Historical Novels for Children,' *History Workshop Journal, 1*, 154–65.

Des (1975) *A Language for Life* (The Bullock Report). London: HMSO.

Jones, A. and Mulford, J., Eds. (1971) *Children Using Language: An Approach to English in the Primary School.* London: Oxford University Press.

Martin, N., et al. (1976) *Writing and Learning Across the Curriculum 11—16.* London: Ward Lock Educational.

Ministry of Education (1944) *Educational Reconstruction.* London: HMSO.

Naughton, W. (1957) *One Small Boy.* London: Macgibbon and Kee.

O'Brien, R. (1973) *Mrs. Frisby and the Rats of NIMH.* Harmondsworth: Penguin Books/Puffin.

Rosen, H. and Rosen, C. (1973) *The Language of Primary School Children.* Harmondsworth: Penguin Books.

Schools Council/Nate (1975) *Children as Readers: The Roles of Literature in the Primary and Secondary School* (Unpublished Report).

Thompson, D., Ed. (1969) *Directions in the Teaching of English*. London: Cambridge University Press.

White, E. B. (1963) *Charlorre's Web*. Harmondsworth: Penguin Books/Puffin.

Whitehead, F. S., et al. (1975) *Children's Reading Interests* (Schools Council Working Paper, No. 52). London: Evans/Methuen Educational.

5

Reading for Learning in the Secondary School

ERIC LUNZER and TERRY DOLAN

PRELIMINARY CONSIDERATIONS

Despite the fashion for such phrases as 'reading growth' or 'reading maturity', instruction in the first *R* has always figured prominently in the infant and junior school curriculum. No one believes that reading comes by itself, by a process of natural unfolding, depending only on the pupil's developmental state of readiness. However, once the pupil has been taught the skills of reading to a level that enables him to give an accurate vocal rendering of a fairly undemanding text (corresponding to a 'reading age' of about nine), it is relatively unusual in Great Britain for him to receive any further instruction in how to read. He is not taught how to deploy the skill effectively, whether for enjoyment or for learning. Should he receive such teaching? Or is the effective use of reading a function of general intellectual development and relatively unresponsive to specific instruction?

The question is not wholly rhetorical, for there is indeed a dearth of research in the teaching of reading beyond the initial stages. Burnet (1971) commented that 'research on reading comprehension is not now being published in quantity nor has it accumulated through the years in massive amounts.' The position has not greatly altered since then, and a recent search through the ERIC (a computer-based index of research in education) records revealed only forty titles reporting research in comprehension in the last ten years. Many of these are specialized, dealing with such topics as the usefulness of illustrations or of 'advance organizers'. Nor is it the case that all attempts to improve comprehension by means of specific teaching have proved successful. The use of *cloze* exercises, for example, as a means of enhancing a critical or thoughtful approach to reading proved ineffective in two studies involving junior college or older school pupils (Phillips, 1973; Ellington, 1972). On the other hand, the majority of American and British studies testify to the success of laboratory materials, especially with average and below-average readers up to at least the age of fifteen (Fawcett, 1977).

Speed and comprehension

There is also evidence that rate training in younger children (at least until the age of ten) can produce improved comprehension as well as improvement in speed (Thomas, 1972). However, McConkie (1972) found that students who were encouraged to read quickly were able to recall less well what they had read than students who were instructed to slow down so as to be able to answer questions correctly. What is certain is that the very high speeds claimed after speed reading courses for adults can be achieved only at the expense of loss in comprehension (Harris, 1968). Indeed, one may seriously question in what sense reading at rates of 1000 words per minute can be called reading; it is a kind of skimming (Graf, 1973).

One is not surprised that rate of reading and comprehension are to some extent positively correlated. Both reflect previous learning. Nor is it surprising that very rapid reading leads to loss in comprehension or in 'information uptake'. It is more surprising that deliberate efforts to increase reading speed can in some cases produce improved comprehension. Can it be that sluggish decoding actually impedes the reader's flow of thought? At present we simply cannot say. But it is a hypothesis that can be tested by suitable experimentation. It is also a plausible one. One might begin by making it a little more precise.

Effective reading

Reading involves two processes: the reader must establish what the
writer has said and he must follow what the writer meant. In
principle, these are quite distinct; the object of the first is the
linguistic 'form' of the text — what the words are and how they are
put together, while the object of the second is its referent, that is, an
idea, thing or event, either in the real world or in an imaginary
world, which the writer has referred to.

However, when circumstances are favourable, the two demands of
reading can be met simultaneously. There is no need to pause at
every word or at each phrase or even at the conclusion of each
sentence in order to make a conscious transition from what is said to
what is meant. Indeed there is now a considerable body of research
to indicate that word identification is partly sustained by the
continuous apprehension of meaning. Both the meaning of what
went before and its form help the reader to determine what comes
next. He can guess at a word when he must (when the text is
damaged or when it takes the form of a cloze exercise); and when he
does not need to, he identifies it more quickly, by combining graphic
cues with grammatic and syntactic ones (see Smith 1973; Gibson
and Levin, 1975). However, when circumstances are less favourable,
one might reasonably suppose that the discovery of meaning, or
some part of it, can occur only after the identification of words but
before the words have been dropped from short-term memory. The
reader who reads too slowly may forget what he has read before he
gets round to making sense of it.

Whether or not this interpretation is correct, we may guess that
one of the most important differences between good readers and
poor readers must lie in the greater pertinacity of the former. Good
readers are more willing to persist in the search after meaning even
when the going gets tough. They are more aware that decoding is
not enough. To that extent their reading is more purposive. They
tend to ask questions ahead of what they read, anticipating what
they may expect to find. In this connection, we may note that the
most widely used reading laboratory schemes, such as the SRA
(Science Research Associates) reading laboratories, lay considerable stress on the SQ3R method of reading ('survey-question-
read-recite-review'). Is the effect of laboratory work mainly to
promote a greater purposiveness in the reader? If so, cannot the same

ends be achieved by other means less remote from the school curriculum and less demanding on the pupil's time?

Programmes for reading

We have already noted that there have been comparatively few studies of the effectiveness of reading programmes, and those that exist do not allow one to draw firm conclusions about what sorts of programmes are successful and why. Nevertheless, a reconsideration of some of the main theoretical and methodological issues in the light of recent research may be valuable. This will be one of the central objects of this chapter. It should enable us at least to make some enlightened guesses about the ways in which future research can help to establish an adequate theoretical basis for making decisions about changes in practice. Our final section begins with a discussion of the kinds of activities that are most worth trying in schools and includes a brief description of a teaching technique that is gaining in popularity as a result of the development work undertaken by the British Schools Council Project on the Effective Use of Reading, together with its associated schools.

READING, COMPREHENSION AND LEARNING

Thinking while reading

Reading is an activity that one does; comprehension is understanding something that one does. For instance, a reader who understands what he has read can answer questions about it, or he can reproduce the gist of it in the form of a written or spoken summary. Even while reading, he can demonstrate his comprehension by supplying missing words, as in a cloze test. If asked to read aloud, his comprehension can be manifest to a tester by the appropriateness of his intonation. All of these procedures have been used as tests of reading comprehension, and while none of them is perfect, each has its advantages. On the other hand, if a student is not asked to do any of these things, it does not follow that he fails to understand what he reads. Comprehension is not the doing of these things, although it has a lot to do with the ability to do them. It is not an action nor is it a process, since both take time, and comprehension cannot be assigned a fixed time.

It makes sense to say 'John is reading' or 'John read for ten minutes before lunch.' It makes no sense to say 'John is comprehending' or 'John is understanding.' We can say 'John understands' (*comprehends* sounds foreign in this context but is equally correct), and even 'John understood before lunch' but not, save ironically, 'John understood for ten minutes.' We conclude that comprehension describes an achievement, like winning a race. It is not itself a process, but it does imply a process or activity that is more than just reading in the narrow sense of reorganizing the words and 'following the sense'. There may be a point in time when comprehension is complete (or as complete as it will be) just as there is an instant when the athlete breaks the tape at the end of a race. But comprehension and winning refer at least as much to the process which went before, the reading or the running, as they do to the particular instants of achievement. However, there is a difference. In the case of the athlete, there was only one activity, running, and the winning merely implies something about how the running was done: faster, on average, than the other participants. The reader who finally understands very often does two things in the preceding phase, of which one is certainly reading. The other, which is likely to alternate with reading, is not understanding (which we have just seen to be an unacceptable usage) but, in some sense, thinking. It is because of these considerations that the authors were led to conclude that comprehension is best defined as 'a measure of the pupil's ability and willingness to reflect on whatever it is he is reading' (see Lunzer and Gardner, 1978).

The amount of time that the reader will need to spend in thinking as opposed to reading will depend on a number of factors. These must include: the readability of the text, its logical/historical structure, the familiarity of its content and frame of reference, and the reader's own purposes in consulting it. We will need to make a short comment on each of these in turn. But to begin with it is worth considering what is known about the relationship between reading and thinking. In this paper, we will use the term 'reading style' to denote the way in which the reader integrates his thinking with his reading.

Observation of reading style

It may seem obvious that a student who is reading a difficult text must take time off to think every now and then. There is now some evidence that poor readers are less likely to do so than are good readers, and that a student can often learn to read more effectively by being made aware of these pauses, even to the extent of introducing them deliberately. Thomas and Augstein (1972, 1976) describe their 'reading recorder,' which has now also been used to advantage by others (Moone, 1976; Fawcett, 1977). The reading recorder enables one to assess the quality of reading directly in terms of variations in the speed of reading (including pauses for reflection) and of backtracking to check on a previous point. The text to be read is mounted on a roller and viewed through a window that exposes three or four lines at a time. The reader turns the roller on when he wants, and he can also turn it back if necessary. The movements of the roller provide an index of variations in reading style. They are recorded automatically by a pen that traces a graph of roller movements in one axis and time elapsed in the other (see Figure 5.1, after Thomas and Augstein, 1972.)

It will be apparent from the pattern of pauses, that there is a continuous increase in the amount of thinking while reading evidenced by the successive traces illustrated in Figure 5.1. However, it should not be assumed that slow reading, frequent pauses and regression or double reading (going over passages twice) are always a feature of effective reading. Thomas and his associates found that students at a College of Education generally altered their style of reading as a result of a programme designed to encourage better study skills, but the changes were not always the same for all students.

Both Thomas and Moone found that the weaker students failed to take in as much as they might unless their reading style included regression or a double read, while the better students performed well in tests of comprehension or recall regardless of their individual reading styles. Fawcett, working with primary school pupils, found that children who were expecting to produce a summary were more likely to read passages twice or to go back to an earlier point than those who were expecting set questions. It may be that junior and younger secondary readers are rarely successful when tackling a difficult passage unless they 'backtrack' or 'repeat', but this has yet to be shown.

The reading recorder enables one to monitor the reading while it is happening. That is its advantage as compared with the comprehension test. It can be useful to the researcher, especially to investigate the interrelation of reading (in the narrow sense of

1. Rapid read, indicated graphically as:

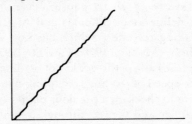

2. Rapid read with stops or hesitations at certain words or phrases:

3. Slow read:

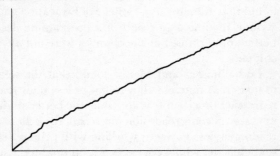

4. Slow read with stops or hesitations:

Figure **5.1** Patterns of reading

5. Double read (generally one of the reads
   would be a quicker one than the other):

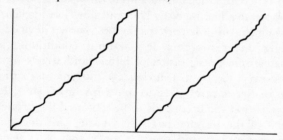

6. Regressed read (reference back to a
   previous section):

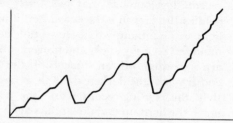

7. Double regressed read (not achieved in
   this research):

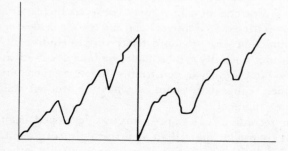

decoding) and various kinds of thinking — for example, clarifying a phrase whose meaning is obscure, comparing what has just been read with something that was read before or is recalled from elsewhere, verifying a point, rehearsing an argument or a sequence of events, perhaps in anticipation of a request to summarize, and so on. However, while the reading recorder can be used by researchers to study the factors affecting flexibility, it was constructed in the first place as an aid to teaching. It enables the student to examine his own study habits in consultation with a counsellor and to answer such questions as: Where did the student stop to think? Why? Where might he have stopped to advantage? Did he read slowly or too fast?

Thomas's Reading Recorder is perhaps the best known device for monitoring reading under more or less natural conditions (as opposed to tachistoscopic presentation of letters and words on a slide or a cathode ray tube or to tracking eye-movements with a camera when the reader is rarely free to move his head, etc.). Its main disadvantage is that the text needs to be mounted on a roller, and the movement of the passage past the viewing slot does not allow the eye movement up and down a page that is a usual characteristic of book reading. Whalley (1977) describes a more recent development that has fewer limitations. Here the reader studies the text in a darkened booth using an oblong beam from a light to illuminate whatever section he wants to read. The light is mounted on a joy stick, and movements both up/down and right/left are recorded on an image of the book-opening. Despite the constraint of the darkened booth, it creates a more realistic situation than the reading/recorder and the reader is much more likely to move the light up and down the page for quick confirmation than he is to move a roller back and forth when using Thomas's apparatus.

Yet another method was devised by Pugh (1978). Pugh's apparatus consists of a specially constructed reading stand that enables the viewer (researcher or counsellor) to observe the reader's eyes (unobtrusively reflected on a mirror) and the text he is looking at. If used in conjunction with standard telerecording equipment, the course of the reader's activity can be made available for study at leisure. This method imposes fewer constraints than any other, but provides a less finely calibrated record of what the student was reading at any given moment.

Like the reading recorder, Pugh's apparatus was developed as an aid to the student counsellor more than as a research instrument. However, all the techniques mentioned can be used for either purpose. Whalley's apparatus has the greatest potential for the researcher, but would need more development before it could be generally usable. At the other extreme, Pugh's reading stand is perhaps more immediately helpful to the counsellor than it is to the researcher. To the best of our knowledge, none of these devices has as yet been used by teachers in a school setting over a long period. Clearly, there is scope for the establishing of reading centres in at least some schools, under the charge of a teacher/adviser of the sort envisaged by the Bullock Report (DES, 1975).

Readability

We referred earlier to some of the variables that might affect what the reader does when he refers to a book and proceeds to read it. One such factor, we have seen, is the sophistication of the reader. Efficient students know when they must stop and think and when they may not. How can we assist the student to become more efficient? To answer that question, we need to say a word about the remaining factors.

The first is readability. Readability is a measure of the style of a piece of writing. It is not a sufficient measure of text difficulty, but it does predict quite well the judgements of teachers and pupils, and it does so objectively. All readability measures are based on two sorts of counts: the number of words per sentence, which is an indirect measure of syntactic complexity, and the frequency of words which are long or rare − a measure of vocabulary demand. To assess the readability level of any text, it is usual to sample at least three 100-word passages taken at random. The best measures of readability (e.g., the Dale-Chall index) correlate at the level of $0.6 - 0.8$ with the averaged judgements of groups of teachers and pupils (Harrison, 1978).

The Effective Use of Reading Project found that not all teachers were especially good judges of text difficulty. Those who were, produced average rankings of passages that could not be bettered by any readability formula when measured against pupil estimates. On the other hand, the calculation of readability can be done by one teacher for one book at a time as and when required, while subjective assessors would find their task much more difficult if they had to give an absolute grading to one passage, instead of ranking several. Thus readability measures are useful to teachers when selecting books for their students. Experiments have shown that pupils answer more questions correctly about a passage written in an easy style than they do when the content is similar but the style is more difficult (see Klare, 1975).

It seems likely that readability is particularly important when the material is in the form of worksheets or workbooks which the student is expected to cope with unaided. On the other hand, writing material that is at once clear, intelligible and readable is a skill that is often hard-won. Writing to a formula, using short sentences and a stereotyped style, may well lead to stifled and even incoherent prose without reducing the severity of the reader's task (see Harrison, 1978).

While the wise teacher will certainly take readability into account when ordering new books, it is clearly not the only important factor. For readability is a measure of style, and takes no account of content or presentation. Also, recent work has shown that readability varies much more widely than was once thought within the same school text (see Stokes, 1978). It follows that either the students must be equipped with techniques that will help them to cope with more demanding texts than one would choose for them, or the teacher must be careful to help them to learn from the written material as and when this is set as a task for classwork or homework. Needless to say, these prescriptions are not mutually exclusive.

Content and structure

There can be little doubt that just as the difficulty of a passage is affected by the style in which it is written, so too the difficulty will be a function of content and structure. To begin with, the reader has more to learn and assimilate if the material is new to him, and also if it is dense. The first point is so obvious that it hardly needs labouring, but the second, which is closely related, is one that might well repay more detailed investigation. Thus the term *dense* denotes a number of features of text, every one of which may well be important. One is economy of writing which, although a stylistic feature, is not measured very well by readability formulae. In particular, one may ask under what conditions even the brevity of sentences becomes an obstacle to comprehension, as in epigrammatic writing. The writing is also less dense when it incorporates several examples to illustrate any generalization, when the examples are spelled out in detail, and so on. Granted that the proliferation of examples and even of illustrative anecdotes helps to make a text more readable, is the essential material also more learnable, or more memorable, or do some students fasten on the vivid and the concrete and fail to pick out the essentials?

These and allied questions point to the importance of such features as the abstractness of the material and the complexity of its structure. Consider the following two passages:

(1) Leeside school is large, mixed and multiracial. Forty per cent of its pupils are English and the rest are second generation immigrants drawn from 26 nations, speaking 21 languages. From his intimate knowledge of the area, the headmaster said that the long established prejudice by white people towards the immigrants generally had not up to the present time been superseded by a polarisation of black and white.

(2) The widely accepted importance of the problems of race relations has led to the extensive study of intergroup prejudice from various points of view. In this field there are economic determinists, frustration-aggression theorists, character structure theorists, personality theorists and many others.

(1) is concerned with prejudice in a single school while (2) deals with theories about prejudice in general. In (1) the people concerned are defined by their relation to a given school; for example, headmaster and pupils, while in (2) they are defined by the type of theory that they espouse. The grammatical subjects of the three sentences in (1) are the school, the pupils, the headmaster. By contrast, the first sentence in (2) is of the form: 'The importance of . . . had led to the study of . . . .' 'Importance' and 'study' would usually be classified as abstract, while 'head', 'school' and 'pupils' would be concrete.

These two passages are discussed by Peel (1974) in the course of a paper that suggests a way of measuring both the abstractness of a text and the level of generalization at which it is written. Peel offers an index based on a classification of all the nouns in a sample passage, on each of the two dimensions of generality and abstraction.

Several criticisms might be made of this work. Peel's concept of abstraction is too narrow, his definitions are sometimes ambiguous, and there is no evidence of their reliability. Above all, we still require objective evidence of the importance of abstraction/generalization as a factor in passage difficulty. Nevertheless, Peel's work is an important contribution in that it opens up the possibility of advance in what is otherwise a somewhat intractable area.

The structure of a passage is yet another aspect that must affect ease of reading but, like abstraction and generality of theme, it is easier to recognize than it is to define or to measure and control. One might surmise that the sequences that are easiest to assimilate are (a) a natural sequence of events, or (b) a list of objects or ideas which are taken to be analogous instances of one and the same thing. Presumably, flashbacks in historical narrative can be as confusing as in film. Even more demanding is the substitution of a more or less complex logical structure for the more primitive narrative. However, attempts that have so far been made to arrive at an objective assessment of the structure of discourse have not as yet resulted in an objective technique that can command wide acceptance. The work of Freedle and Carroll (1972) contains several contributions that highlight the problems of adequate description in this area, but precisely for that reason, the methods that are offered are too time-consuming to be of much general value.

The teacher may be more fortunate than the researcher here. For there are techniques that are too inaccurate to be of use to the researcher, but which can nevertheless be very serviceable to the student and counsellor. Thus Thomas and Augstein (1976) claim considerable success for a method of counselling that includes the production of flow diagrams to represent the logical structure of any passage under study. The method is less than objective, so that no one graphic description of a text can claim to be definitive, but the process of constructing his own description and comparing it with someone else's may well be a powerful stimulus and aid to the student. In the end, we would like to be satisfied by properly conducted experimentation that such activities are indeed beneficial, but the *prima facie* case is a strong one and may well be sufficient for many teachers.

We have already seen that readability alone accounts for much of the difficulty of text as reported by teachers and pupils. Nevertheless it may be that factors such as structure and abstractness are more insidious because they are less easily noticed and therefore less often compensated by re-reading or by reflection. One may speculate that young readers are more likely to notice an obscurity associated with low readability than one which is due to the abstractness of the content or to complexity in arrangement. This would follow from the fact that low readability hinders word recognition as well as immediate apprehension of syntactic sense, while difficulties of content and arrangement are a barrier only to fuller understanding. This last conclusion is described as speculation, since it has not been confirmed in research. For it goes without saying that more complex arrangement and more abstract content are nearly always associated with lower readability. Further research is clearly necessary, using artificially constructed texts, so that the various factors can be examined independently of one another.

Suiting reading style to reading purpose

It has often been said that the most important consideration for a person's style of reading should be his own purpose. A student may read a passage to prepare for an examination or a test; or he may be reading it out of general interest, or to clear up a particular point, or for sheer enjoyment, or simply to pass the time. Nor are these categories exhaustive, for each admits of further subdivision. For instance, a different style of reading is required for revising material that is familiar or for mastering ideas that are new.

There is ample evidence that readers are affected by the kinds of questions they anticipate they may have to answer (see Rothkopf, 1966, 1968, 1972). Thomas and Augstein (1972) were able to show further that students who were preparing to write an abstract of a passage were as good as or better than others at answering set questions, even though the others had prepared to answer questions. The latter were greatly inferior at writing abstracts.

Clearly, then, the reader's pupose does affect what he can do after he has finished reading, so presumably it must affect what he does when he is actually reading. Indeed, we saw evidence earlier that readers preparing for an abstract are more likely to backtrack. However, such research is limited in that the purpose is set by someone else and follow-up is usually immediate. Can it be that the difficulties that face the reader are compounded when neither the time nor the passage to be read has been pre-set and when there has been no arrangement for an immediate follow-up? It is highly probable that this is indeed so, and, once again, Thomas and Augstein (1976) offer evidence that students (in a College of Education) are more often uncertain as to their purpose in reading before entering a study skills program, and are less often uncertain thereafter.

Over the past ten years, there has been an increasing tendency in English secondary education to extend the methods and ideas of primary education at least into the first and second years of the comprehensive school, including mixed ability grouping and the encouragement of project work. It is probably true to say that a thoroughgoing commitment to such an ideal is rare, and there was little evidence of it in a not unrepresentative sample of six schools in which observations were made in studies on behalf of the Schools Council Project on the Effective Use of Reading (see Chapter Four in Lunzer and Gardner, 1978). However, it is by no means difficult to find work of this kind going on (Chapter Six, ibid.). What is perhaps disturbing in the light of the foregoing discussion is that in neither setting is adequate guidance given to young readers about how to read and how to study.

There is a suggestion from one study that good readers differ from poor readers mainly in their ability to profit from reading material that does not hold their interest (see Shnayer, 1969). In this experiment, readers were asked to answer questions about a variety of passages, all of which made heavy demands on them in terms of readability. However, they were also asked to rate the passages for interest. It was found that poor comprehenders answered questions as well as the better readers on passages they had rated as interesting but that their performance slumped on passages rated as dull. Once again, one is left to surmise that reading for meaning is mainly a matter of asking questions of the text — and of course of finding answers. Even the poor reader will do so when he is made to — for instance, when answering easy questions with the text in front of him, or when his interest is sufficiently roused.

Most of the researches to which we have referred offer indirect evidence that the good reader knows how and when to vary his style of reading, and that the poor reader can be helped to do so. However, while few would doubt the importance of such flexibility in reading, it must not be thought that it is easy to measure, so that pupils who score highly can be left to fend for themselves and others can be given remedial aid. A comprehensive review of such studies by Rankin (1974) shows the difficulty of accurate measurement in this area.

To pick out the flexible reader from the less flexible is difficult (after allowing for more 'superficial' differences such as overall reading efficiency as measured by a standard test such as the Gates-MacGinitie). To attempt to select specific weaknesses in comprehension is to pursue a chimera. Such is the conclusion to which we and our associates have been led after careful study of the relevant literature (see especially Farr, 1971) and a committed attempt on our part to reach an opposite conclusion (Lunzer, Waite and Dolan, 1978). There is no evidence that some pupils can be reliably shown to be good at picking out the essential points of a passage, but bad at drawing inferences, or good at the interpretation of metaphor, but weak at discovering the particular meanings of words and phrases in a given context. All these are evidence of the 'ability and willingness to reflect on the matter that one has read,' and it is these tendencies that the concerned teacher will wish to develop and encourage. There is no support in our research for the attempt to develop separate 'skills' of the kind just referred to.

In particular, the several attempts to derive distinct factors to represent five to ten or more putative sub-skills have either failed to do so, or they fail to agree with one another as to the nature of these factors. The best known attempt, and the one most often quoted in support of an opposite conclusion (Davis, 1962) provides evidence only of a general comprehension factor, a vocabulary factor (closely related) and a literature/non-fiction factor. (For fuller discussion see Lunzer, Waite and Dolan, 1978.)

While it is futile to attempt a programme of remedial education designed to promote fictitious sub-skills, it does not follow that programmes of reading should exclude requests to list the main points of a passage, or to interpret a metaphorical phrase, or to draw legitimate inferences from statements given in the text. These are all appropriate questions to ask, and in answering them pupils must look more closely at the text and recognize its possible meanings. Such comprehension exercises constitute one way of promoting more careful reading.

INNOVATIONS IN SCHOOL PRACTICE

Whose responsibility?

Central to the conclusions of the Bullock Committee was the notion that one can bring about a significant improvement in standards across the curriculum by paying more attention to the development of greater language competence in all four modes: listening, speaking, reading and writing. Our own belief is that whatever differences one finds in the language of children — and of adults —

are at least as much *reflections* of differences in knowledge, in interests, and in attitude as they are causes of such differences (see Lunzer and Dolan, 1977; Lunzer, Dolan and Wilkinson, 1976). At the same time, any attempt to bring about improvement in the language of learning is also likely to induce a change in the relevant knowledge and attitudes. Indeed, because we regard thinking and knowledge as more critical than language, we welcome the stress that is laid on talking and listening as against an over-emphasis on writing. While writing complements reading in a logical sense, it by no means follows that all useful reading should lead to writing. Indeed, if reading is to be a vehicle of learning as well as a stimulus to learning, it is essential for schools to entertain a more imaginative approach to the possibilities of 'self informing' together with the kinds of follow-up that it permits.

There are, however, a number of problems that every school will encounter as soon as it seeks to implement the recommendations of the Bullock Report as they relate to language in general and reading in particular. The first major difficulty is that of selecting the most appropriate curriculum strategy. Should the staff of a school make a concerted, across-the-curriculum effort, or should the responsibility of improving children's reading rest with one school department?

There are advantages and disadvantages on both sides. Subject teachers may rightly claim that effective reading is most meaningfully developed in the context of a specific content area. In this connection, they might point to the importance of introducing pupils to the special terminology and nomenclature of subject disciplines, sometimes referred to as their specific register.

The word 'base' for example, has different meanings in mathematics, chemistry and music, while the child who is asked for 'the solution' by a chemistry teacher needs to ascertain whether an answer to a problem is required or whether a liquid with a solid dissolved in it is referred to.

Usually, however, subject teachers will feel that helping the average pupil with problems of reading demands specialized knowledge that is perhaps available to the remedial teacher but is lacking in themselves. For instance, how does one teach a boy or girl to look at the passage as a whole in order to decide on the most probable meaning of a particular word or phrase? If this kind of problem becomes more intrusive, as it will do when children are asked to use their reading as a vehicle of learning, subject teachers may feel that their time can be better spent instructing their own discipline than trying to patch up the work that should properly have been done in the primary school.

Again, it will be said that children need to be taught how to make the best use of indexes and headings in books, dictionaries and encyclopedias, library catalogues, referencing systems in resource areas and so forth. Many of these will be common to several fields of study if not to all. To that extent it seems wasteful to replicate the programme for each school department.

Most commonly one finds a compromise. All members of staff are expected to cope with any reading problems that arise in lessons while the development of literacy skills is entrusted either to the English Department, or, more rarely, to the Remedial Department. All too often, however, this means that the programme is inadequate. Reference was made earlier to differences in register that may obtain between one subject and another. But the greatest differences are those that separate literary usage, scientific usage, business usage and everyday usage. Teachers of English will often occupy themselves with the first, the third and the fourth. One can hardly blame them for neglecting the second, when there are others who possess the necessary specialization and experience. It is difficult to envisage a situation in which the teacher of English was thought to be the right person to teach students how to study chemistry — or even history (though here the gulf is less wide). Also, the emphasis in teaching English usage is more often on writing than it is on reading. Again, since time is limited, the choice seems inevitable. For the pupils will, in time, be judged by the adequacy of their own writing, and there is much to learn. Inadequacy in reading is less obvious, precisely because comprehension is a private affair.

In the first section of this paper, reference is made to the work of Fawcett which indicates that, properly used, the SRA reading laboratories can lead to measurable gains in comprehension at all ages up to at least fifteen, and although the weaker pupils benefit most, there are gains among abler students as well (Fawcett, 1977; Lunzer and Gardner, 1978). Nevertheless, the approach of this scheme is in some ways a narrow one, with an over-emphasis on a particular style of reading, SQ3R, over-reliance on a particular kind of question (the sort that admits of objective scoring, and is therefore often less searching than one could wish), and insufficient attention to the different demands and challenges contained in different reading material across the range of fiction and non-fiction.

The recent introduction into British schools of the Scott Foresman Reading Systems programme heralds the arrival of total reading schemes. These comprise a complete set of reading materials and supporting apparatus, starting at pre-reading level and going through to the level of applied sophisticated reading for children in the secondary school. These schemes, although comprehensive and thoughtfully produced, are expensive. Predictably, this has prompted teachers to adopt what seems to be a well favoured strategy in British schools — that of picking out bits of commercially produced schemes to supplement, or even to feature centrally, in home-produced programmes. SRA reading laboratories are often used in this manner rather than in the systematic and regular pattern intended by their designers.

It seems likely, therefore, that some schools, albeit a minority, capitalize on the availability of tried reading schemes and develop programmes to promote learning through reading under the auspices of a single department, usually English. One might predict that when they depart from the recommendations of the framers of those programmes, their best chance of success will be in enlisting the collaboration of colleagues in a variety of departments.

Already, however, there are schools that have chosen the alternative course of involving all departments from the start, so that reading for learning becomes a part of learning itself, rather than an ancillary activity. Here one must guard against the several departments in a school electing to pursue policies which are not only different, but in some sense contradictory rather than complementary. Our own experience through the project on the effective use of reading leads us to suggest that a greater unity of purpose can be achieved by capitalizing on the potential of group discussion as an alternative to writing, for following up and consolidating the knowledge gained in reading.

Group discussion as an adjunct to reading

How much time do pupils spend on reading in the course of the secondary school day? When they read, what sorts of texts are they concentrating on and what is it they are being expected to do? These questions were investigated first by Squires and Applebee (1969) and more recently by Dolan, Harrison and Gardner (1978). It seems that up to 17% of the pupil's time may involve him in some reading, although the reading is rarely continuous and the amount of reading varies from one subject to another. In regard to the second point, it appears that most often reading is called for in short bursts rather than as continuous activity, and reading usually occurs in conjunction with writing. It seems to be the case that pupils are rarely asked to 'read in order to learn'. When they do read, they are more often reading to find out what to write.

Such over-emphasis on writing as a follow-up to reading can be counter-productive. For children's ability to read thoughtfully is often greater than their written work would suggest. Equally, the ability to write well is a fairly weak indicator of children's ability to discuss with intelligence what has been read. Indeed, children are often in a far better position to write once they have discussed with each other an assignment set in print. Stauffer (1969) and Walker (1974) have described a set of activities intended to lead children to flexibility in their reading of texts and passages encountered in different subject areas. Essentially, the activities involve small groups of children in reading to solve problems, to discuss solutions and to reflect not only on the results of their reading and discussion, but on the thinking and strategies used in arriving at decisions. The following are three typical activities:

Group Prediction

Group prediction exercises involve releasing instalments of a short passage, one at a time, to a group of 8–12 readers. The task is to respond to questions put by a group chairman (at first a teacher, but later, as the group gains experience, one of the group), the questions being directed at finding out what is significant in the text and at anticipating what might happen in later instalments. All reading is silent and no writing is involved. Following reading and discussion of each instalment, the chairman collects the instalments so that no back reference is possible. Readers are encouraged to justify their responses, and other members of the group are encouraged to challenge the responses.

Group Sequencing

For this exercise a passage is photocopied and cut into sections that are stuck onto card for greater durability. Working in pairs, children are encouraged to try to work out the author's original order, although it may be stressed that the pair must explain the reasons for their decisions to each other, and try to reach agreement. If possible, this exercise should be followed by an opportunity for two, three or four pairs to compare and discuss their findings, and to discuss any discrepancies in predicting the author's order. It is suggested that 6–12 cards be used, and that cards with less than twenty words not be used too frequently.

Group Cloze

In this activity, participants read a passage in which every nth word has been deleted. No constraints are laid down in relation to passage content or length. Deletions may be every fifth, seventh, or tenth word, depending on the difficulty of the passage and the nature of the audience. Deletions should not be commenced until about the hundredth word. Sub-groups of two, three or four children prepare their answers, with stress being laid on the need for convincing argument within the group before decisions are reached. The chairman (usually this will be the teacher at first, but ideally the role should be taken by others) calls the subgroups together to compose a final version. The chairman possesses the original version, but must try to avoid notions of 'right' and 'wrong'.

These techniques were taken up by our own teams and further developed with more particular reference to their potential in the secondary school. (See Dolan, Dolan, Taylor, Shoreland and Harrison, 1978. Group discussion techniques are also currently used by Dolan and his associates in teaching adult literacy classes.) Previously, these techniques were used largely if not exclusively with younger children and mainly as an instrument to be used by the reading specialist.

Our own approach has been to initiate suggestions that have then been taken up by subject teachers with remarkable effect. By way of example, the following 'group sequencing' exercise was prepared as a revision procedure for a group of CSE entry pupils who had just completed a series of lessons on the topic of digestion.

The pupils are given six cards, bearing the labels *oesophagus, stomach, mouth, duodenum, large intestine, small intestine*. These are in random order and the first task is to place the 'headings' in the order of their functioning as food is processed by the digestive system. This ordering is done in pairs, and when it is complete, two or three pairs of students will come together to compare their respective orderings. Finally, the teacher checks the listing for the entire class. Pupils are then given the following pieces of information:

Food goes through the digestive system

(1) The waste material contains quite a lot of water which is useful to the body, so this is absorbed through the walls of the digestive system and into the blood. Peristalsis again causes the material, now much drier, to be passed along the digestive tract and finally passed out in defaecation.

(2) This great length is needed to allow the completely digested food to be absorbed through the walls of the digestive tract. The whole process of digestion has been for the purpose of converting food into particles small enough to pass out of the digestive tract and into the blood stream in this way.

(3) Here it is pushed down towards the stomach by a process called peristalsis, which consists of muscular contractions passing down the tube.

(4) Eventually the food is passed into the   . Here the walls of the digestive system are much thicker and more muscular than elsewhere, and the food is churned up into a soup-like consistency and is called chyme.

(5) At this point the acidity of the chyme is neutralized and bile is poured onto the food to break down fat into small droplets ready for digestion. This is because fat digestion begins here, and the digestion of protein and carbohydrates is continued because of the secretion of a number of different kinds of digestive juices from the pancreas.

(6) While digestion is being completed the food passes along the ileum or   . It is so called because it is small in width, but it is not small in length, forming a coiled tube several yards in length.

(7) When the food is sufficiently soft it is formed into a bolus and passed into the   , a tube-like structure.

(8) The large pieces are broken down to small pieces by means of the teeth. In addition, saliva is poured into the food to soften it and to start the breakdown of sugars into smaller pieces (molecules).

(9) After absorption is completed, any waste materials are passed into the

(10) When food is placed in the   and first taken into the digestive system, two things happen to it.

(11) After a time, by the relaxation of a muscle which closes off the stomach (the pyloric sphincter), the food is allowed to pass bit by bit into the

(12) At the same time, acid is poured onto the food, along with a digestive juice which begins the breakdown of proteins (fish, meat, eggs).

Once again, the task is to order these correctly, by allocating two of the cards to each of the headings already established. The method of work is the same as before, separate pairs coming together for disucssion after first attempting to reach independent solutions.

In one instance, new partnerships of children were established to repeat the exercise a second time. It was interesting to note that on the second trial, although the exercise took a shorter time to complete, discussion was fuller — all children were ready, equipped with one solution and a set of justifications. In all, the exercise took twelve minutes, leaving the teacher plenty of time to discuss the passage with the children and to sort out any misunderstandings.

The activity certainly alerted the teacher to several inconsistencies and misunderstandings in the learning that had taken place prior to the exercise. One interesting reaction was to the word 'eventually' in item 4. Some children were misled by the word, since they felt that it signified the end of a very lengthy sequence; they argued that it couldn't possibly refer to the stomach as this was relatively early in the process of digestion. The teacher noted that many such misunderstandings were adequately resolved in the course of the exercise.

The example above may be sufficient to illustrate the value of this kind of activity, in which the written word occupies a central place, yet the object of the lesson is clear throughout. The pupils taking part are reading in order to learn. Learning to read is incidental, as also is learning to learn, if indeed consciousness of either object is present at all.

Nevertheless, we must conclude on a note of caution. As indicated above, it is by no means certain that the thinking that is involved in the course of group reading activities carries over into the student's private study reading. Indeed, every one of the activities implies a structuring on the part of the teacher who sets the problem and 'doctors' the text, so that the student is made to think. A great deal of further exploration will be needed before one is in a position to make any confident assertions about the place of this sort of work in the general curriculum. Presumably, the use of highly structured activities involving 'doctored' passages must be followed up with others in which the students are given greater freedom to ask their own questions and to impose their own structures on the text.

Finally, more thought will need to be given to ways in which work of this kind can be made instrumental in leading students to making appropriate decisions about their own purpose when reading in general. For we have stressed throughout this chapter that different styles of reading suit different occasions.

References

Ausubel, D. (1968) *Educational Psychology, a Cognitive View*. New York: Holt, Rinehart and Winston.

Burnett, T. W. (1971) 'Research on reading comprehension: implications for the elementary teacher,' In *Reading Methods and Teacher Improvement*, Smith, N. B., Ed. Newark, Delaware: International Reading Association.

Davis, F. B. (1968) 'Research in comprehension in reading,' *Reading Research Quarterly, 3*, 499–545.

Des (1975) *A Language for Life* (The Bullock Report). London: HMSO.

Dolan, T., Dolan, E., Taylor, V., Shoreland, J. and Harrison, C. (1978) 'Improving reading through group discussion activities,' In *The Effective Use of Reading*, Lunzer, E. A. and Gardner, K., Eds. London: Heinemann.

Dolan, T., Harrison, C. and Gardner, K. (1978) 'The incidence and context of reading in the classroom,' In *The Effective Use of Reading*, Lunzer, E. A. and Gardner, K., Eds. London: Heinemann.

Ellington, B. J. (1972) *Evaluation of the Cloze Procedure as a Teaching Device for Improving Reading Comprehension*. Ed. D. thesis, University of Georgia.

Farr, R. (1969) *Reading: What can be Measured?* (An IRA Research Fund Monograph for the ERIC/CRIER Reading Review Series). Newark, Delaware: International Reading Association.

Fawcett, R. (1977) *The Use of Reading Laboratories and Other Procedures in Promoting Effective Reading Among Pupils Aged 9–15*. Ph.D. thesis, Nottingham University.

Freedle, O. and Carroll, J. B. (1972) *Language Comprehension and the Acquisition of Knowledge*. Washington, D.C.: Winston.

Gibson, E. J. and Levin, H. (1975) *The Psychology of Reading*. Cambridge, Mass.: The MIT Press.

Graf, R. G. (1973). 'Speed reading: remember the tortoise,' *Psychology Today, 7*, 112–3.

Harris, A. J. (1968). 'Research in some aspects of comprehension: rate, flexibility and study skills,' *Journal of Reading, 11*, 205–10 and 258–60.

Harrison, C. (1978). 'Assessing the readability of school texts,' In *The Effective Use of Reading*, Lunzer, E. A. and Gardner, K., Eds. London: Heinemann.

Klare, G. R. (1975). *The Measurement of Readability*. Ames, Iowa: Iowa State University Press.

Lunzer, E. A., and Dolan, T. (1977) *Making Sense* (Report to the Social Science Research Council).

Lunzer, E. A., Dolan, T. and Wilkinson, J. E. (1976) 'The effectiveness of measures of operativity, language and short term memory in the prediction of reading and mathematical understanding,' *British Journal of Educational Psychology, 46*, 295–305.

Lunzer, E. A. and Gardner, K., Eds. (1978) *The Effective Use of Reading.* London: Heinemann.

Lunzer, E. A., Waite, M. and Dolan, T. (1978) 'Comprehension and comprehension tests,' in *The Effective Use of Reading* Lunzer, E. A. and Gardner, K., Eds. London: Heinemann.

McConkie, G. W. (1972) 'Experimental manipulation of reading strategies.' (Paper presented to the American Educational Research Association, Chicago, Illinois).

Moone, J. (1976). 'Some thoughts on study skills,' *Reading, 10*, No. 3, 24–34.

Peel, E. A. (1974). 'A measure of the generality — abstractness of a text.' (Unpublished paper, Birmingham University).

Phillips, B. D. (1973). *The Effects of the Cloze Procedure on Content Achievement and Reading Skills in a Junior College Introduction to Business Course.* Ph.D. thesis, University of Northern Colorado.

Pugh, A. K. (1978) *Silent Reading: An Introduction to its Study and Teaching.* London: Heinemann Educational.

Rankin, E. F. (1974) *The Measurement of Reading Flexibility* (Reading Information Series: *Where do we go?).* Newark, Delaware: International Reading Association.

Rothkopf, E. Z. (1966) 'Learning from written instructive materials: an exploration of the control of inspection behaviour by test-like events,' *American Educational Research Journal, 3*, 241–9.

Rothkopf, E. Z. (1968) 'Two scientific approaches to the management of instruction,' In *Learning Research and School Subjects* Gagne, R. M. and Gephart, W. J., Eds. Itasco, Illinois: Peacock.

Rothkopf, E. Z. (1972) 'Structural test features and the control of processes in learning from written material,' In *Language Comprehension and the Acquisition of Knowledge*, Freedle, O. and Carroll, J. B., Eds. New York: Wiley.

Shnayer, S. W. (1969) 'Relationships between reading interest and reading comprehension.' In *Reading and Realism*, Figurel, J. A., Ed. Newark, Delaware: International Reading Association.

Smith, F. (1973) *Psycholinguistics and Reading.* New York: Holt, Rinehart and Winston.

Squire, J. R. and Applebee, R. (1969) *Teaching English in the United Kingdom: A Comparative Study.* Champaign, Illinois: National Council for the Teaching of English.

Stauffer, R. G. (1969) *Teaching Reading as a Thinking Process*. New York: Harper and Row.

Stokes, A. (1978) 'The reliability of reading formulae,' *Journal of Research in Reading, 1*, 21–34.

Thomas, L. and Augstein, S. (1972), 'An experimental approach to learning from written material,' *Research in Education, 8*, 28–46.

Thomas, L. and Augstein, S. (1976) *The Self-Organised Learner and the Printed Word* (Report to the Social Science Research Council).

Thomas, S. L. (1972) *An Analysis of Reading Rate Improvement Program in Grades Two, Four and Six*. Ed. D. thesis, Montana State University.

Walker, C. (1974) *Reading Development and Extension*. London: Ward Lock Educational.

Whalley, P. C. (1977) 'Aspects of purposive reading, the analysis of reading records,' (Paper presented to the Annual Conference of the British Psychological Society, Exeter).

6

Literature in the Secondary School

BERNARD HARRISON

Many of the books which now crowd the world, may be justly suspected to be written for the sake of some invisible order of beings, for surely they are of no use to any of the corporeal inhabitants of this world. Of the productions of the last bounteous year, how many can be said to serve any purpose of use or pleasure? The only end of writing is to enable the reader the better to enjoy life; or better to endure it.
(Samuel Johnson, Review of Soame Jenyns' *A Free Enquiry into the Nature and Origin of Evil*)

In order to inculcate and develop a love of literature in his pupils the teacher should treat it as a form of art in which literature is the communication of zest, and this is possible only if the pieces selected are those which the teacher can read with full enjoyment. Commentary should be used solely as a means of heightening the pleasure of great literature, of explaining the content where explanation is needed.
(*The Education of the Adolescent*, The Hadow Report, 1927)

The passages quoted above help to show that there is nothing very new about the main views to be advanced in this chapter: that reading and response to literature should be enjoyable experiences, that engender a sense of a richer, deeper meaning to living. These views may seem, perhaps, to be only more obviously true of literature (to which the passage from the Hadow Report limits itself), than to be true of *all* reading, to which Samuel Johnson's memorable polemic extends.

Few English teachers would deny, I venture, that it is in literature, above all in poetry, where language is seen to carry the amplest and most vivid feeling and meaning; we turn to novelists, poets, playwrights for the richest and most deeply enjoyable interpretations of life through language. The central importance of literature in the teaching of the mother tongue ought to be, and often is, assured, in our schools. But there is perhaps some danger in the present climate of discussion of being over-cautious (and yet of being thought over-contentious) in making claims for the place of literature, and its powers to influence human growth through language in the young learner. It is difficult to recall any really serious, explicit attacks over the last ten years or so on the principle that the teaching of literature is of central importance; on the other hand, the sheer weight of attention that has been given to other aspects of language study has diminished the amount and the quality of attention that was, say, being given a decade ago to teaching and learning through literature. The Bullock Report itself (DES, 1975) — which set out first to investigate the learning and teaching of reading — echoes the Hadow Report passage, if somewhat hollowly, in its insistence that reading is not just a mechanical business of identifying shapes and sounds, but is intimately linked with processes of thinking and feeling. But its actual attention to literature is limited to a meagre fourteen pages (from over six hundred); and well written though this chapter of the report is, it must be admitted that it makes little impact on the mainstream subjects of the report, or even to the section of the report on reading, to which it is tucked away as an endpiece. Such over-modesty (or undervaluation?) may tempt the teacher of literature to make over-aggressive claims for the importance and value of literary studies in schools. Aggression is a necessary element of persuasion; but I should wish to avoid such polemic here, in the belief and hope that the importance and value of literary studies are still held to be self-evident and widely accepted in schools, and that it will be more appropriate to try to raise and consider some issues that may help to *refresh* good principles and practice in the teaching of literature, in the light of recent emphases and insights into the learning and teaching of the mother-tongue.

Literature, culture and relationships

In an essay on 'Education and Culture', Tolstoy defines culture as
the 'free relation' of people. The notion of culture as a 'free relation'
will predominate in this chapter, in its exploration of the
contribution that literature may make to 'culture'; it will not be so
much concerned with notions of 'cultural heritage', 'cultural levels',
or the cultural backgrounds of different social classes. Tolstoy's
version of culture leads us, usefully, to consider the actual, living
culture that develops among the people of a particular classroom. It
takes both pupils and teachers as they are for its starting point, and
it accepts Sapir's declaration (1934) that:

> There is a very real hurt done to our understanding of culture when we
> systematically ignore the individual and his types of interrelationship
> with other individuals.

As teachers, we are coming increasingly to recognize that it is in
this area of 'interrelationship' where the most significant and
characteristically human qualities may be nurtured and developed
— where individual identity may grow and flourish from the roots of
a well defined and vigorous cultural identity. Applying such a view
to the teaching of literature, F. R. Leavis (1962) has suggested that
we might do well to envisage a 'third realm', where the literary work
is re-created in reading and collaborative discussion among a group
of students, so that the 'collaborative-creative' process of discussion
and growing response gives us a

> living whole that can have its life only in the living present, in the
> creative response of individuals, who collaboratively renew and
> perpetuate what they participate in — a cultural community or
> consciousness. More, it gives us the nature in general of what I have
> called the 'third realm' to which all that makes us human belongs.

Such a view has underpinned much of the most interesting recent
writing on the teaching of literature in schools. Marjorie Hourd, one
of the most distinguished of such writers, has revised an earlier book
with the new title of *Relationship in Learning* (1972), in which she
suggests that the practising teacher needs 'to know more of how the
imagination works in terms of the self and other people at one and
the same time'. Miss Hourd then suggests that there are signs of

what should be regarded as a healthy movement towards more subtle forms of teacher 'guidance', where the emphasis is more and more on 'directed expression of thought and feeling in a self-chosen medium', rather than on the acquiring of techniques and standards, though these will still have their place. Robert Witkin (1974) emphatically agrees that the trend *should* be that way, but offers evidence to suggest that there may not be much cause for optimism, at least in the literary classes he observed as part of a notable Schools Council study on 'Arts and the Adolescent', which the directed (his work will be referred to later). The American writer Alan Purves has suggested, in a refreshing set of 'notes on a response-centred curriculum' in the teaching of literature (1972), that:

> At the centre of the curriculum are not the works of Literature, or the individual Psyche, but all the lines connecting the two — the mind as it meets the book — the response.

This response, he declares, is 'a sense of knowing, a sense of feeling, a sense of moving-in-me' all of which coalesce to give a 'kind of pleasure, a sense of the fitness of things'. The rest of Purves' practical and useful book shows that where a class is concerned, such a relationship need not be confined to the individual reader and the book. When a class is reading and collaborating on books together, then each book that is read may come to mark a new phase in the relationship that is being formed among the people in that class; and individual responses to the book become bound up with this. *SAY* (1969), by a practising schoolteacher, Simon Stuart, illustrates this process well, so that a successful lesson is summed up thus:

> The whole lesson demonstrates the interaction of literary exploration with the personal relations of the set. Sometimes the relations pull the purely intellectual pursuit out of true, sometimes they inspire discoveries; and this works both ways — the literary discoveries create a greater understanding of the personal relationships.

The view and quality of life that a book represents come to be bound up in the relationships and culture of the class, and to contribute to the values and outlook of that group.

To meet the work of literature in this way, and to weigh it against life's realities, is no easy task. It might even be said to be the truly difficult and only truly worthwhile form of literary criticism; for as the playwright Ionesco (1964) once asked of his ideal critic-reader, the reader is required both to be himself and to renounce himself, as fully as possible, in order to give full recognition to a book. But this is an advanced and ideal version of a response; relationships with books, as with people, grow only gradually, and cannot be compelled or hurried, since they come wholly from the *free* engagement of the learner. The analogy of 'relating to books' with 'relating to people' may be usefully pursued in considering the earlier phases of reading response. At certain times the pupil may seem to use a book (as he may 'use' a flexible and patient teacher/parent/counsellor) for his own immediate, esoteric needs, to 'sound out' his own fantasies, anxieties and desires through wish-fulfilment or identification with a character. Such a phase in a literary or a human relationship would often come before a fully recognizing and reciprocal 'friendship'. The early phases of response may not seem to have much to do with the 'focal' meaning or identity of the book, but they may be of considerable personal value to the reader and perhaps to his whole peer group — just as in human relationships, a 'giving' partner might allow himself to be seen and used in a particularly restricted light for particular purposes, offering a role of confidant, for instance. Arguably, a book may be adapted for this kind of use with less compunction than may be necessary where actual people are involved; and such a special, dependent relationship might be the best, or indeed the only, way towards more mature and balanced appreciation of the book, and of other books, in good time.

The 'world' of a satisfying book may offer, then, a special kind of dependable relationship, which the dependent one can trust and take for granted, while finding the resources and courage to explore the world for himself, in his own directions. A book that offers the chance of a living relationship with its reader offers support and release; and this may be as true of the reluctant reader's comics as it is of a work of Solzhenitzyn or Shakespeare's *The Winter's Tale*. Thus the learner will develop 'standards' of enjoyment and meaningfulness in reading, according to his own personal needs and intimations. These earlier phases of response may have the same kind of correspondence with the world of ideas and understanding that an infant's 'transitional object' (D. Winnicott's term, 1971) such as a teddy bear might have with the forming of living relationships outside the self; the early phase is a highly necessary prelude to later phases of recognition and relationship.

At best, then, reading and responding to literature are movements towards intimacy. A reader becomes more aware of his own personal, private self and feelings; he is also 'taken outside himself', through encounter with the book, and through hearing and contributing to the responses of other readers (Leavis's 'collaborative-creative process'). He learns to develop a dialectical (inner-and-outer) rather than an unbalanced solipsistic-subjective, or imposed 'objective' view of the world with which he seeks relationship; and this process can take place only in the 'third realm', that potentially creative space between the learner and the outside world. In that area the learner can bring personal difficulties, confusions or moral issues into clearer focus, while at the same time they can be freed from his involved self, and therefore become less threatening and alarming. As a privileged spectator/receiver in a special (at first, probably exploiting) relationship, the reader can observe and reflect on his chosen issues, but with less personal stress and discomfort than he might feel when actually living through the raw and immediate experiences of life.

To take a familiar example of this process from literature: in Blake's poem 'The Poison Tree', the reader recognizes the poet's admission of hateful and poisonously mean feeling, and in seeing the source of those feelings clearly, as potentially a part of his own inescapably human make-up, he is made disconcertingly aware of the intense satisfaction to be gained from acting out a hateful feeling. On the other hand, he sees that to avow such real and intense feeling, and to bring it into the light of other, different feelings (in this case these are indicated in part by the contemplative, sober tone of the poem) is in itself a relief, so that the reader may wonder more 'coolly' about whether it really is best to nurture and justify hateful feeling. The feeling comes to be seen and understood for what it is; and it is also distanced, and more easily dealt with *critically*. The poem has become a point of growth, rather than an agent of suppression, in its 'moral' effect. In Rollo May's terms (1967) the act of recognition and relationship through reading has transformed 'neurotic' (disabling) feelings of guilt and anxiety into the 'normal' (growth-promoting) feelings of guilt and anxiety that are needed to quicken and develop the moral sense of the living individual. Thus the literary text has played its part in developing powerful and valid insights into life; free response has been stimulated, and has grown towards responsibility.

Further notes on creative response

So far, my argument has depended a good deal on that brief definition by Tolstoy of culture as 'free relation', in order to suggest that there are deeply personal, autonomous aspects of the learner's reading and response that must be respected by the teacher, and that there are very important reasons why reading and response should be seen as a shared, collaborative process. The teacher himself has an obligation to provide appropriate books, ideas, lines of investigation, that will develop the 'creative space' of the learner. Reading, like all other aspects of language activity, has a social basis, in which the reader's response involves subtle adjustments to, and subtle adjustments of, word meanings. The Bullock Report itself points out that even at very elementary levels of reading, the reader is involved in the rudiments of critical and creative feeling and thought-processes, relating what he is reading to his own life and experiences, to what he already knows. In offering distinctions between primary, intermediate and comprehensive reading skills, the report suggests

> The most effective teaching of reading is that which gives the pupil the various skills he needs to make the fullest possible use of *context clues* in searching for meaning.

There need to be many meeting points between experience of life and experience in books; and the sensitive teacher of literature will always be obliged to spend a good deal of time and ingenuity in choosing the right sources at the right time for his pupils, in order to foster their creative responses and growth. Without that sense of faith that the book will somehow relate to him and his world, the individual will naturally have no motive to make the effort himself to relate. It is important to recall that, although the Bullock Report concluded that there was no general evidence available to support suggestions that standards of reading had either risen or declined, it found evidence of 'a rising proportion of poor readers among semi-skilled and unskilled workers' in decaying inner-city areas —

among the most potentially alienated groups in our community, in fact. And while Bullock's findings may not give an overall discouraging view of general reading attainments, a distinctly less comforting picture emerges from a recent report that particularly concerned itself with 'English lesson' kinds of reading in schools. The recent Schools Council work on *Children's Reading Interests* (Whitehead *et al.*, 1975, 1977) reveals from its extensive survey into British secondary school children's reading habits and choices that 36% of children of fourteen and over read no books at all by choice (although 29% of those read comics). This figure, taken with Bullock's warning note about the rising proportion of poor readers among the children of disadvantaged groups, might be taken together to suggest a significant growth of alienation from reading for pleasure, at least among a sizeable part of the community.

Anyone involved in the teaching or bringing up of adolescents will recognize that whatever difficulties or exasperations they experience in their encounters with and learning about adult life, there is no doubt of their powerful drive to relate, unless sickness intervenes. That a fourteen-year-old should choose something or someone to relate to, other than a book — a friend, a television programme, a walk around the town — need not give rise to concern, unless we find that he has chosen not to read through frustration in his attempts to read and be involved. If, for instance, school text-books have given him no pleasure and little sense of profit, he is not likely to have been encouraged to venture out into making his own reading choices. He needs to be able to feel that the book really does offer a world for him to inherit; and the teacher may justify exerting pressure on him to read only if he has good reasons for believing that the reading experience will in fact be liberating and strengthening. What Paulo Freire (1973) has declared about a literacy programme may be held to be equally true of a literary programme. Freire has described how he and his co-workers in Brazil sought to identify words and phrases that carried the greatest emotional force and meaning for his students, and how they then proceeded to build a literacy programme round them. In Freire's view:

> Literacy makes sense only in these terms, as the consequence of men's beginning to reflect on their own capacity for reflection, about the world, their position in the world, about their work, about their power to transform the world, about the encounter of consciousness — about literacy itself, which thereby ceases to be something external and

becomes a part of them, comes as a creation from them. I can see validity only in a literacy programme in which men understand words in their true significance: as a force to transform the world. As illiterate men discover the relativity of ignorance and wisdom they destroy one of the myths by which false élites have manipulated them.

This passage offers a forceful reminder that considerations about reading, as with considerations of other aspects of language activity, cannot be separated for long from much wider issues of culture, of men's feelings and their capacity for action. The quality of our response to literature helps to condition, and is conditioned by, our capacity to respond creatively and critically to the world in which we live, a world which shapes us, and which we may help to shape in turn.

Growth towards feeling-insight

Perhaps it should be made clear that my intention in quoting Freire above is not to suggest that all young readers of literature should become political activists overnight; but rather, that as they come gradually to inherit power of various kinds in their lives, they should do so from their own individual, creative-critical centres, not as 'impressed' people. As far as teaching literature is concerned, a vital early need in youth — indeed a vital need at any age or degree of sophistication — is for the reader to be clear about what he really does feel, in response to what he needs.

Robert Witkin has written a valuable study on the difficulties and vulnerabilities to be experienced by the learner in his search to progress from what Witkin has termed the 'sensate problem' (in the case of literature, whatever text, scene or image that quickened his feeling-interest) into a full resolution of his feeling-idea, through talking, or writing, or whatever form he has chosen. Yet Witkin found that on the evidence of the (let it be admitted, limited) literature classes that he observed, very little was happening that could be fairly described as involved with the feeling-response of the learners. He recorded that while self-expression and imaginative work were considered by the teachers he interviewed to be high priorities in their lessons, in fact much more emphasis was placed on 'objectivity' and the growing ability of the adolescent pupil to handle generalized and abstract language — an emphasis which, Witkin suggested, disregards the equally important fact that adolescence is a period of

> stirring emotionalism, of shifts of affect, the discovery of passion and embrace of commitment, of undying love of absolutes and total involvement.

He records too his suspicions of 'critical' approaches that are demanded especially at A-level and that tend to cut between a student and his full *subjective* response to a book or poem. The expression of feeling, he declares, thrives on a 'controlled subjectivity', rather than on exclusive objectivity, and

> if the price of discovering the subjective feeling states of others is the sacrifice of one's own subjectivity then the step has truly been a retrograde one and from the point of view of self as well as self-expression it might be argued that the pupil is better off with the naive egocentrism of childhood.

In underlining the need for subjective response by the learner, Witkin also declared that a further inhibiting factor against its realization in schools is a general fear of the 'live wire' power of emotion. The teacher is tempted to withdraw from the difficult and delicate business of recognizing his own, or the learner-reader's feeling-preoccupations; he prefers instead to offer depersonalized, 'objective' formulations of literature, which come in turn to be approved of as 'grown-up' modes of expression when they are borrowed by the learner. The thousands of possible ways of response to a literary text may thus be repressed by such directive and limiting teaching tactics. If the teacher wishes to encourage truly creative-critical thought, he must decide how he can best aid and guide the pupil's own 'reflexive response', to use Witkin's phrase.

In what has since become a celebrated example of a good teaching approach to literature, John Dixon (1967) offers a transcript of a lesson in which a group of fourth-year pupils are discussing Lawrence's poem 'Last Lesson in the Afternoon'. This transcript offers an excellent, if brief, view of a group of learners gradually and naturally finding their own way into a new experience (the poem) supported by tactful and stimulating intervention from the teacher. The teacher who has learned to wait for a class to respond to a literary text, as well as deliberately to prompt and probe, will recognize the promise and value in the approach that Dixon recommends. After reading, say, Blake's 'Little Boy Lost', there may be a short silence, which is broken by someone offering the comment that some teachers still wear gowns for lessons in the comprehensive school down the road (echoing the 'gown' of the priest in the poem). Such a response may be accepted as being a more likely sign of the true interest in the material before the class, than, say, passively waiting for the teacher to ask his first question on the 'meaning' of some phrase or line would be. An exploration has begun, based on a first and, one might add, by no means irrelevant response to the poem.

While the class may gain a good deal from a flow of queries and suggestions from the teacher, it is strictly *their* encounter with the material and with any guidelines offered that is to be of importance. Later, the class might insist on a direct contribution from the teacher, and will themselves turn 'Socratic', querying 'Why did you choose this poem?', 'What do these first two lines mean, anyway?', 'They don't make sense, do they?', and so on. A direction from the teacher to think definitively too early on 'meaning' or 'quality' might well inhibit this growth-process; identification of the text grows only slowly from the learner's first wondering and wandering responses. An initial leisureliness and sense of occasion when encountering fresh work may be the most appropriate way into more sustained and rigorous enquiry at later stages. In this way, a class can be encouraged to realize that even when the new experience is felt to be understood clearly, one's sense of its place and significance may still develop and change.

An illustration of what these early stages of subjective response may be like is some writing by a girl in a mixed ability class (fourth year) about Blake's poem 'The Human Abstract'. It is a poem that may well present considerable difficulties and confusions to a sophisticated adult reader, and is not necessarily recommended as a 'good choice' of poem for a mixed ability fourth-year class; neither is the girl's piece of writing offered as being in any way a 'model' of how the reader should respond to this poem. It is offered, rather, to illustrate how a member of a class that has been encouraged to respond personally, to write freely and adventurously, and to solicit help from the teacher as *they* require, comes to choose and take on a task that might well daunt a mature student of literature. This poem and its companion poem 'The Divine Image' had been read in class, and they were asked, after some discussion, to choose from several writing topics, one of which was to write on the 'pictures' or images that the 'Human Abstract' presented to the mind's eye.

What I saw in the poem

This poem "The Human Abstract" is a difficult poem to judge and understand. It only means what you want and believe it to mean. What it means to you, anybody else would disagree entirely. To someone else they would put an entirely different context to you. Not everyone is the same, minds are different and minds work differently. Everyone has a different character and the poem, I suppose, is analysed according to your character. If you had a cruel character, you probably won't take too seriously to the lines "Then cruelty knits a snare And spreads his baits with care."

There again, if you had a soft "easily-dented" character, you probably wouldn't take these lines too softly, you'd think about them, chop them about and put them into different context.

When you, Mr. H. read the classes essays you'd expect everyone's essay to be different, every one in our class has a different character, Tom's or Stephen's characters aren't the same as Kim's or Sally's, four completely different essays.

> Pity would be no more
> If we did not make a somebody poor.

Those two lines, the first two of the poem, if everybody was rich, no-one would need to take pity on anyone else. But then the world would rebuilt entirely on greed. Everybody would want more and more there would be utter chaos and greedy people getting greedier and greedier.

> Then cruelty knits a snare
> And spreads his baits with care.

What do you think these two sentences mean? I think that they are talking about a poacher who carefully knits a web of snares and traps. Then he carefully baits the snares. Or perhaps it symbolizes a spider creating a web, spreading its web, its bait with care. All set and ready to catch its dinner. Humility takes a root underneath its foot. Humility is trodden in, ground in. A mystery a dangling web which spreads over the dismal shade. Or perhaps the mystery is hanging over the caterpillar or fly. The caterpillar and the fly feed on mystery. What mystery, the mystery of the "Human Abstract."

The mystery bears the fruit of deceit, he says, all ruddy and sweet to eat. The mystery all ready to feed on. The thickest shade, rather like the dismal shade with a mystery, and Raven made his nest in the thickest shade of tree. So, the thickest, dismal shade, the mystery where the Raven builds its nest.

The gods of the earth and the sun looked and searched for the tree that the Raven built its nest in. But their search is all in vain as there is a tree growing in the human brain. The tree of knowledge.

Amanda, aged 15

Amanda has chosen to take on a very complex poem here (she could have opted for a less taxing assignment, but particularly wanted to do this). Her hesitant, meandering approach clearly suggests 'thinking aloud' through her writing, and there is no serious attempt to make this a 'finished piece'. After several digressions, in which she offers a few defensive thoughts about her own possible misunderstandings, she begins to wrestle with the meanings of the lines; and while revealing some understandable confusion over the first two lines of the poem, she begins to form a clearer picture of subsequent lines. At this point she shows that she wants to enter into a dialogue, and brings two lines to her reader, saying 'what do you think these two sentences mean?' But then she returns more and more to Blake's original words, phrasing and nightmare imagery, and simply 'tells the story' of the poem, almost in Blake's words. But that this is an involved and wondering closeness, rather than merely mechanical repetition, is shown by her final phrase, which goes straight back to the very heart of the poem. She shows more confusion than understanding overall, and cannot be said to be thinking logically here; on the other hand, she *is* thinking, in that she is wondering, trying to connect, exploring the images, and she is prepared to admit her confusions to the reader/teacher, to show where she might benefit from further help. In Witkin's phrasing, she is beginning to move towards identifying a 'sensate problem', towards 'feeling-thought'.

Blake does not give his reader much help in this poem; it is indeed a richly imagined vision, which seems to have more to do with dream-symbolism than with discursive reality. The poet's intention seems to be to disturb and engage the feelings at a subconscious level, so that he must then patiently wait and explore the inward response that has been made. It is not a poem that lends itself easily to 'small group' discussion, for instance, until some preliminary personal reflections have been worked through. In fact the writing of the class offered a 'pool' of ideas for some further work, on this occasion; and Amanda's suggestions about the poacher in particular offered a useful contribution to this. Thus, it may be seen how a literary work offers a rich and significant construct of reality, in this case through Blake's eyes. But the aim of the teacher is not so much the 'literary-critical' one of appreciation of the forms (although some pupils may develop a specialist interest here), as to offer the pupils a way towards the encounter of inner self with outer life. The poem was chosen to aim very directly at their feeling-response, to offer them possible connections, which would disturb them into forming a 'sensate problem'. In this way a connection was sought with their as yet unadmitted inner, personal experience and intimations, in order to enable a process of bringing that experience into clearer focus. It is readily admitted that the poem is not the happiest choice that might be made for such a class; but the poem helps to show that erring in the direction of more, rather than less, difficulty might result in richer learning and teaching than a poem that might be more obviously near to the learner's mundane existence.

That the concern for 'personal experience' in teaching is sometimes misunderstood was well indicated by Jerome Bruner in *Towards a Theory of Instruction* (1966):

> The personalization of knowledge [is] getting to know the child's feelings, fantasies, and values with one's lessons. A generation ago, the progressive movement urged that knowledge be related to a child's own experience and brought out of the realm of empty abstractions. A good idea was translated into banalities about the home, then the friendly postman and trashman, then the community, and so on. It is a poor way to compete with the child's own dreams and mysteries.

The teacher, in helping the learner to encounter his 'own dreams and mysteries' (which may become itself a deeply educative experience for the teacher) can help to show how human wisdom, insight, knowledge, is an organic thing, in which all men may be seriously and creatively involved. A poem such as 'The Human Abstract' helps to bring the learner to

> realise, then, that the artist is someone who, like yourself, has been plunged into this confusing world without his consent; someone who, like yourself, must find his way willy-nilly among the welter of things below. (Paul Klee, in Grohmann, 1954)

Symbol-making: a concluding note

Coleridge, who defined the creative-understanding process as being brought about by the 'esemplastic powers of the Imagination' shows beautifully in 'The Ancient Mariner' how new growth is brought about by the fresh play of imagination. The Mariner has been jolted, through terrible experiences, from his blindly greedy and exploiting relationships in life. He is removed from zestful living, and suffers morbid, anguished depression through his own guilt feelings. But gradually, after prolonged suffering, he learns to celebrate, with a child's vision, the loveliness and meaningfulness of what had formerly seemed ugly to him; and he describes how the colour, shape and movement of the water-snakes captivate him, so that in his fresh admiration and love for them he came to 'bless them unaware'. That new, naïve response marks the beginning of the Mariner's new growth of being and awareness. Such a quality of response (the Mariner's, that is, rather than the highly sophisticated religious and moral insight of the poet himself, as revealed in the poem) is characteristic of children's best responses to literature, at those points where they have been moved into full involvement with a text. It is in the realized form of literature that they are offered the fullest possibilities of language, and where they may have the best opportunities for developing their own capacity to form meaning through symbolic association.

An impressive essay in this field has been published by Majorie Hourd (1974). Miss Hourd refers to Adrian Stokes and Marion Milner as being among the very few writers who have attempted to treat psychoanalytic concepts under the heading of creative thinking; and after reviewing some insights in this area from a number of major creative writers and from the writing of children, she suggests that what the post-Romantic literary tradition has called 'imagination', and what twentieth-century thinkers and psychoanalysts have called 'symbol-formation' may be usefully regarded as intimately connected terms. She goes on to declare:

> If we regard symbol formation as a continuous process of bringing together and integrating the internal and external early and later experiences we can appreciate the force of Melanie Klein's remark that 'symbolization is the basis of all talents,' that is, the basis of those skills by which we relate ourselves to the world around us.

It follows, as she herself concludes after a dense and persuasive argument, that those who 'have no capacity for symbol formation are indeed sick as well as inarticulate', and that these include:

> Young children for whom play spells anxiety rather than a natural joy and a necessity; and older children to whom the symbol is a threat in as far as it is a link between inner and outer, for they cannot believe that they have firm footing in either world . . .

The capacity to respond to literature — at first, perhaps, to be able to ransack it on his own terms, then later to achieve empathetic response to the writer's otherness — enables the reader to endow himself with a store of language and experience that is already richly charged with meaning. It is difficult to imagine a better way of establishing a foot in both 'worlds' than through the study of literature.

References

Bruner, J. S. (1966) *Towards a Theory of Instruction*. Cambridge, Mass.: Harvard University Press.

Creber, J. W. P. (1965) *Sense and Sensitivity*. London: University of London Press.

Des (1975) *A Language for Life* (The Bullock Report). London: HMSO.

Dixon, J. (1967) *Growth Through English*. London: NATE/Oxford University Press (Second Edition, 1975).

Freire, P. (1973) *Education for Critical Consciousness*. London: Steel and Ward.

Grohmann, W. (1954) *Paul Klee*. London: Lund Humphries.

Hourd, M. (1972) *Relationship in Learning*. London: Heinemann.

Hourd, M. (1974) 'On creative thinking,' *Tract*, No. 13.

Ionesco, E. (1964) 'The writer and his problems,' *Encounter* (September), 3–15.

Leavis, F. R. (1962) 'Two cultures?' (The Richmond Lecture), *The Spectator*, (March 9th), no. 6976, 297–303.

May, R. (1967) *Psychology and the Human Dilemma*. Princeton, New Jersey: Van Nostrand.

Purves, A. (1972) *How Porcupines Make Love: Notes on a Response-Centered Curriculum*. Chicago, Illinois: Xerox Corporation, University of Illinois.

Sapir, E. (1934) 'The emergence of the concept of personality in a study of cultures,' In *Selected Writings of Edward Sapir*, Mandelbaum, G. D., Ed. California: University of California Press (1949).

Stuart, S. (1969) *SAY: An Experiment in Learning*. London: Nelson.

Tolstoy, L. (1862) 'Education and culture,' In *Tolstoy on Education*, Wiener, L. Chicago: University of Chicago Press (1967).

Whitehead, F. S., *et al.* (1975) *Children's Reading Interests* (Schools Council Working Paper, No. 52). London: Evans/Methuen Educational.

Whitehead, F. S., *et al* (1977) *Children and their Books*. London: Macmillan Education.

Winnicott, D. W. (1971) *Playing and Reality*. London: Tavistock.

Witkin, R. (1974) *The Intelligence of Feeling*. London: Heinemann.

7

Putting it into Practice — Language and Learning in the Secondary School

MIKE TORBE

The widespread interest expressed in the ideas of 'language across the curriculum' since the publication of the Bullock Report has been paralleled by an equally widespread confusion about what that phrase means, and even more about what a language and learning policy is. I have tried elsewhere (Torbe, 1976) to explain what a language and learning policy is. Here I want to consider the question of what such a policy looks like when it is operating in a British secondary school. I run the risk of appearing to generalize from limited examples, but I believe this is justifiable. I am trying to synthesize the good practice that I have witnessed and that I myself believe in into a composite image of what learning and teaching could be like. I contend that there is a family likeness visible between teachers of any subject whose practice sets out to make a language and learning policy operational; their practice sets out to lead inevitably to learning and understanding, rather than rote remembering, whatever the subject. (The theory that I will be drawing upon to underpin the descriptions of practice is deeply indebted to the following: Barnes, 1971, 1976; Barnes and Shemilt,

1974; Britton, 1970; Dixon, 1974; Martin, et al., 1976; Rosen, 1967, 1971, and others.)

The crucial point to make about a language and learning policy in operation is that, on the whole, it does not differ from conventional teaching in its stated aims. The ability to present writing that is publicly acceptable and the ability to control, understand and select from relevant knowledge are still major priorities. I hope to illustrate how it does differ *in the way it sets out to achieve those aims.*

To start then from the fundamental plank of language policy: the intention of all teaching is that pupils shall not only possess information but shall understand and be able to select from and use that information. But pupils can remain unaffected by that information unless they become conscious of their own intellectual and emotional relationship with it. Therefore, teachers are always searching for ways of enabling their pupils to approach new information and make it their own within a language and learning policy, so that in a sense, they reconstruct knowledge rather than take over 'preformulated information' (the phrase is from Michael Armstrong, 1973). 'Information' and 'knowledge' are words that are really too positive to be used satisfactorily; at the first stage of acquaintance with a new idea or concept, the response might well be very personal and not apparently directly related to the information itself in any academic way. That is, it may not have the characteristics of formal academic discourse. For instance, here are four examples of pupils making the first tentative steps into understanding in their own terms. (Except when otherwise stated, the pupils are in mixed-ability classes in comprehensive schools in Coventry, England).

(1) A first-year class (12-year-olds) in a humanities lesson have just watched a television film as part of their course on "Children at War". The film ("The Way we used to Live," from YTV) is about a family living through the days leading up to September, 1939. The teacher invites the students to "talk about the most important parts of the film," in small groups. The children, almost unanimously talk, not about the "information," but about how it must have felt to be there and to have experienced the black-out and, above all, evacuation. They talk of how they themselves would react in that situation, and tell each other stories of analogous experiences.

(2) A first-year home economics class is engaged in a series of lessons

about hygiene. The teacher has introduced ideas about bacteria using formal teaching,* and discussed the need for hygiene in the kitchen. As the pupils examine moulds through bioviewers, they comment on how the food looks, reminisce about mouldy food at home, and remind each other of stories they have heard or read about food poisoning.

(3) A fourth-year history class (15-year-olds) is just beginning the study of Mussolini and Hitler. The teacher asks them to talk in small groups of three to four about what they would do if they were dictators. After about fifteen minutes she asks them to decide "who would be the most important people to have on your side if you were a dictator, and who you would need to control". Another ten to fifteen minutes of small-group talk and then, as the teacher draws the classroom discussion together, she feeds into this, as comment on the pupils' ideas, historical information about Hitler, Mussolini and Fascism.

(4) A second-year sixth form group of ten students (age 18) studying A-level English is reading Keats. The teacher provides each group of two to four students with a cassette tape-recorder, and asks them to record themselves talking together about "Ode to Psyche," and to make a note of the important things other people in the group say. After twenty to twenty-five minutes, the group comes together, and shares, very slowly and haltingly, its earliest thoughts about a difficult poem. The teacher listens more than he talks, makes few comments upon the quality of the students' ideas (though he does say at one point, "Oh, I hadn't thought of that"), but takes care to show the group the general points they've made themselves. At the end of the lesson, he asks the group to listen to their tape-recordings during the next week, and to transcribe the most interesting two or three minutes.

In all these cases, the pupils are making the first connections between the new ideas they are meeting, and what they already have in their heads — the map of experience against which they test new experiences. The teacher, who may appear to be having an easy time, and even to have abdicated, is in fact working extremely hard, firstly to set up a situation in which the pupils are able to talk purposefully but freely and easily, and secondly to make evident to

*The teacher recorded the lesson and commented to me afterwards, 'I must have used the word 'bacteria' a hundred times'. As a result of hearing the tape, she fundamentally altered her plans for following lessons.

the pupils the importance of what they are saying themselves, because otherwise they may either not recognize, or may undervalue, the importance of their own utterances. It is hard work, teaching like this, much harder than lecturing or formal exposition. For one thing, keeping quiet because you recognize the importance of the pupils' own formulations, is, as any teacher will agree, very difficult, when the most natural thing is to talk, to correct, to explain and comment. Moreover, in a lecture, the teacher has done the preparatory work, the formulation and organization of his ideas, before he comes to the pupil. He has a pre-ordained path to follow, and invites the pupils to follow the same path. It is much more demanding for a teacher to hold in his head a clear map of the learning territory he is in, but to be tolerant enough to allow decisions to emerge from tentative discussion, and to trust that this learning will be real and powerful for the pupils. He may still lecture, and will probably have to explain, but if he does it later, when the pupils possess a sense of context for that information (rather than at the beginning as a way of presenting new information), the lecture is more likely to be effective.

This teaching is not 'permissive'. The teacher must be constantly on the alert, attuned to what the pupils are trying to articulate, and able to co-operate with pupils rather than dominate them. The teacher can so easily betray the pupils, by disregarding what they say, by undervaluing it, by not building upon it, or worst of all by allowing all the talk to take place and then finally pre-empting it by insisting that the pupils take over the teacher's own interpretation after all. When that happens, the pupils are quick to see that their first tentative formulations are being cheapened. As its best, teaching that encourages this kind of purposeful but tentative talk as the basic building blocks of learning is acting out a theory of learning. The Bullock Report (DES, 1975) expressed it thus:

> It is a confusion of everyday thought that we tend to regard "knowledge" as something that exists independently of someone who knows. "What is known" must in fact be brought to life afresh within every "knower" by his own efforts. To bring knowledge into being is a formulating process, and language is its ordinary means, whether in speaking or writing or the inner monologue of thought. Once it is understood that talking and writing are means to learning, those more obvious truths that we learn also from other people by listening and reading will take on a fuller meaning and fall into a proper perspective.

Nothing has done more to confuse current educational debate than the simplistic notion that "being told" is the polar opposite of "finding out for oneself." In order to accept what is offered when we are told something, we have to have somewhere to put it; and having somewhere to put it means that the framework of past knowledge and experience into which it must fit is adequate as a means of interpreting and apprehending it. Something approximating to "finding out for ourselves" needs therefore to take place if we are to be successfully told. The development of this individual context for a new piece of information, the forging of the links that give it meaning, is a task that we customarily tackle by talking to other people.

The encouragement of purposeful talk among and between pupils is crucial. Pupils remember and learn what they themselves formulate rather than what is presented to them pre-formulated. Some fourth-year pupils commented, for instance, that after discussion they recalled what they themselves had said rather than what the teacher said, even though the teacher's words 'made sense at the time'. But, they added, they also remembered the bits immediately preceding and following their own contributions. Pupils in other schools, my own experience in groups, and research evidence all confirm this.

There are several characteristics of this stage of talking towards formulation that are of importance. The teacher who encourages tentative first-stage thinking in talk is aware, at least intuitively, that its characteristics are not those of public language, and also that it is necessarily very different from writing in its grammar, organization and form. Recognizing the differences between talk and writing he will accept, therefore, talk that is hesitant, unpredictable and anecdotal, because it is a step on the way towards a more polished, formulated, organized and conscious public language. The teacher has to develop ways of monitoring, building upon and reflecting back what the pupils say, so they can see its value. There is, however a constant tension in the teacher, because the decisions any adult has to make about adolescent talk — to intervene or not, to remain silent or to participate — are heightened and made exquisitely complex by his positions *as* a teacher. One is always on the verge of a wrong decision, as the next example shows.

(5) A fourth-year Religious Education lesson in a girls' comprehensive: The class is working in small groups. They have before them a passage about pain and suffering which has been presented to them

in the form of cloze procedure. They are deciding which words are most suitable for the gaps. The teacher eavesdrops on a group of four girls. They are talking about last night's television. Does he interrupt and gently remind them of their task? He agonizes about it, then decides not to intervene. As he listens, one girl says "He was in dreadful pain, wasn't he?" (referring to someone on television). Another answers, "Yes: like down here (in the passage they are reading). What did you say for this word here?" The group returns voluntarily to the assignment.

Trusting that pupils will return to the assignment is so important; but I am conscious that there is no way I can prove to the sceptic that it will happen. The main reason for my saying this is that it is something I have constantly to re-discover for myself, and that I find the decision always difficult. There is an anxiety that makes every lesson like this a venture into the unknown, and the teacher needs a strong will to delay commitment until he can see for certain the direction that pupils' talk is taking. Consider the following transcript as an example, in which the talk is serving purposes imperceptible to the teacher. Four fourth-year girls in an O-level history group are talking about the First World War, and are recording their talk. There is no teacher present. They have shown already on the tape that they are a close group of friends, and that they can both maintain serious discussion and also tolerate apparently digressive witticisms. We join the transcript after twelve minutes of discussion.

(1)	June	You can't really say that we won the First World War, can you?
(2)	Gill	Yes but we didn't lose
(3)	Kath	But we didn't win we just lost as many men as what the *other sides did*
(4)	Karen	*Yes, yes*
(5)	June	I suppose if they hadn't gone the world would be overpopulated now
(6)	Gill	*Yes that's true*

They are still talking seriously; but suddenly, with no preparation, no pause, no change of voice or pace, a curious digression occurs.

(7)	Gill	We had our carpet laid down last night it's lovely
(8)	June	Is it a new one?

(9)	Gill	Mmm
(10)	Kath	A new carpet? What colour?
(11)	Gill	Cream
(12)	June	Green? Got a red one. My new Hoover came yesterday, beautiful, latest style out
(13)	Karen	We've got a red one
(14)	?	Of what?
(15)	June	You want to see it a Hoover, new fashion model, cost £40

Imagine a teacher who happens on the group during utterance (7). Wouldn't he assume that the digression was unprofitable, and request that they return to the 'real' topic? Let us see what actually happens.

(16)	Kath	Yes, but . . .
(17)	Karen	. . . sucker. You said you had your new carpet
(18)	Kath	No, but that's got nothing to do with the war (laughter)
(19)	Karen	Clever

Clearly, Kath at least is holding the agenda for the talk constant. Karen, taken up with her own wit (the Hoover is a 'big sucker') wants to enjoy that a little longer; but then, she herself is triggered by an odd in-joke of Gill's into a memory of something that is worrying and preoccupying her, after her visit to the courts that morning.

(20)	Gill	It comes from the Salvation Army
(21)	?	. . . her new carpet laid
(22)	Karen	There was a man and he didn't have anywhere to live in the courts this morning
(23)	June	In the where?
(24)	Karen	In the courts. Stole money, and he got drunk and he didn't have anywhere to live. He was a tramp.

There have been two digressions: what now? How would a teacher react again to Karen's utterances? More sympathetically, perhaps than to Gill's at (7), but still indicating gently what ought to be discussed. But the girls take over the controlling role themselves.

(25	Gill	What about — O.K. I'll tell you what we can talk about. We can talk about — no I don't think so

(26)	June	What can we talk about then?
(27	Kath	About whether you think murder — in the F. . . . whether you think killing men like you know when you're in the trenches is murder
(28)	Karen	*No, you've just got to defend yourself*
(29)	June	*No, because everybody does it*
(30)	Kath	Because if you didn't do it if they didn't kill you you'd be shot by your own men so you're forced to
(31)	?	Let Juneanne say something, she hasn't said nothing sitting there like a stuffed dummy
(32)	Karen	You've got to defend yourself, though
(33)	Gill	It must have been a hard job for the people in trenches because some of them didn't even know the men they were shooting
(34)	June	Let's discuss propaganda in the First World War

Clearly, the teacher would have been unwise to have been directive. The girls have taken on the responsibility for controlling their own learning, something all teachers hope for in their pupils' behaviour. The discussion continues for a further ten minutes, and this minute or two of talk seems to be the kind of plateau effect often noted by researchers, when serious discussion must be relaxed for a moment before the next surge of intensity. The point is, of course, that in a normal 'disciplined' classroom, where the teacher controls the ebb and flow of classroom discourse, it would simply not be evident to the teacher that the pupils *can* control and monitor their own discussion because they have no opportunity to do so. The acceptance, tolerance and even encouragement of this kind of talk is not easily acquired; initially, one has too many doubts about it. But it is through inspecting tapes and transcripts like this that one learns to respect talk.

Taping and transcriptions demonstrate another aspect of a language and learning policy: the determination to explore what really does go on in the classroom. There is a gap between the memory of what happened and the reality collected so dispassionately by the tape-recorder, which forces one to accept how inaccurate and unconsciously prejudiced one's memories can be. The reliance on memory or on normative assumptions about pupils and classroom experience has been shown conclusively to be misleading (see, in particular, Hargreaves, *et al.*, 1975; Keddie, 1971; Nash, 1973). Judgements about whether learning has or has not taken place turn out to be equally problematic unless they are underpinned by genuine documentation. A teacher who attempts to explore the learning processes that occur in talk in his lessons makes new discoveries about hitherto unnoticed events; the way he talks to his pupils, the authority dominance he can exert, the sheer quantity of his talk, the kinds of question he asks, and the way he may mis-hear, misinterpret, talk across, or simply miss, what pupils say. He also shifts his perspective completely; from being worried about how successfully he is teaching he becomes worried about how successfully he is enabling the pupils to learn.

There is a crucial distinction to be made for teachers between language for communication and language for learning. Put another way, when we use language to find out what we think and feel, we are learning. When we use language to tell others what we think and feel, we are communicating. It is difficult to 'communicate' until we have learned what it is we have to communicate. It is true that there is an inevitable interaction between the two: the act of communication often generates new learning for instance. But I am primarily concerned here with first formulation, when learners encounter and come to terms with new ideas. The perspective on learning through talk I have described applies to writing, too.

Just as important as recognizing that we can learn by talking is recognizing that writing can be a way of learning, as well as a way of expressing what has been learned. The tolerance for expressive talk needs to be extended to written language, so that polished, neat, correct public essays are not seen as the only kind of writing possible. Pupils should be encouraged to recognize that on the way to the polished piece, several other varieties of writing may be used.

(6) A geography teacher in the second year has shown the class a film about the Bushmen of the Kalahari. When it is finished, instead of leading a class discussion, she invites the pupils to write down exactly what they are feeling and thinking. In the few minutes left, they talk to each other in pairs and threes and compare notes. Next lesson she reminds them of their writing, asks them to re-read it and then to link together in pairs or threes to use their notes so that they can make a presentation to the rest of the class about the Bushmen.

(7) The teacher of a fifth-year O-level history class tells the pupils they will be considering note-taking today. He asks the class to work in pairs and for one pupil of the pair to take notes while the teacher reads, and the other to listen and then write afterwards what can be remembered. He reads a passage about the Russian Revolution for

five minutes. There is a pause while the second group writes their version from memory. The pairs compare their versions, consider the differences and similarities in what each considered important, and the strengths and weaknesses of the two approaches. They discuss with the teacher for the last ten minutes their general discoveries about note-taking. The teacher asks them to compile a further version of the passage by synthesizing the notes.

These are conscious attempts to employ different kinds of writing. (This issue is further explored in Britton *et al.*, 1975.) One attempt, in particular, is recognizing the importance of first-draft thoughts written down as a record, without paying too much attention to form or correctness. It is the equivalent in writing of tentative, expressive talk, in the way it allows the pupil to think aloud on paper. This is not to undervalue polished writing; but to capture new ideas on the wing, speed, not propriety, is needed. This is writing for learning; fixing new ideas into language raises into the consciousness what might otherwise have remained latent and unavailable. The later stages of combining these ideas with others, and organizing and reshaping, are important steps towards mastery of complex concepts and their interrelation, and therefore of successful writing in formal modes; but it depends absolutely on a first stage at which the 'finding out what we think and feel' took place.

Writing, then, in the hands of an inventive and thoughtful teacher, who is conscious of language processes, can be a very powerful way of exploring ideas.

(8) A second year science class have just completed a unit on distillation and solutions. The teacher sets a two part test. The first part is a conventional multiple-choice test: the other is simply a sheet of paper that reads:

Chapter 1

It had only taken five minutes for the ship to sink after the fire and the final explosion, but the swim to shore had been agonizingly long. He could not remember losing consciousness, but the hot sun burning into his skin brought him round. He was on a small island. A quick look round showed him there was no one else on the island, and, what was more, no fresh water. Could he survive? He sat for a long time in deep thought.

Chapter 2

In their struggles to complete 'Chapter 2', the pupils reveal most clearly the degree to which they have genuinely understood the science they have learned. Some who score highly on the multiple choice test (where they do not have to make their own formulations) show they really have not grasped the basic principles involved, despite their apparent success, and their stories, although fluent and readable, demonstrate the gaps in the pupils' understanding. In this first case, for instance, a subtle but crucial point — how the distilled water is to be collected — is omitted:

> Then he wondered how he would survive without water, then he had an idea, he could collect a sample of sea water in a weaved basket he could have made quickly. Because the water would fall out of it, he put damp leaves on the end so that if any water should fall out it will soak into the leaves. He then layed it out in the sun then waited until the water evaporated, then the salt would be left. He chucked the salt on the damp leaves away, and put the evaporated water under as much shade as he could and waited 'til it cooled and it would turn into water again. This time it would be clear fresh water. He said, "I can live like this for days," and he waited until a ship came to rescue him.

Others can control and reorganize the information they possess extremely efficiently, and demonstrate genuine understanding.

> Then he went to a bamboo tree and hacked off a branch he then cut this down and hollowed it. Then a bottle floated up with an irony ['ironic', M.T.] letter asked for help. He put the note aside and smashed off the neck of the bottle. Then at bend of a branch he cut at each end of the bend. He then rubbed two sticks together and when it sparked he put the note there and blew lightly, the note set alight and he put it in a pile of wood, the fire went well. He filled the bottle with sea water put the bend over it and the tube attached to that. Then he put a clean rock shaped like a cup there, the flames heated the water, the steam went round in the tube which was surounded by dead wet leaves to keep it cool and the steam went back to water (pure water) which he drank from the rock.

This teacher has recognized that writing can be a process by which learning can occur and be monitored as well as the medium for the product in which knowledge is presented. The conventional modes of writing most frequently found in school, however, can work powerfully against learning, because they put a heavy premium on retelling to the teacher information that the teacher has already given the pupils. Indeed, the *expressive language* — which the Writing Research Unit (Britton, 1975) suggested was the most powerful mode for learning — was also the mode they found least in evidence in British schools. That it can exist without weakening academic learning, and that it can encourage pupils to explore new ideas for themselves, is shown clearly in the work of the Writing across the Curriculum Project (Martin *et al.*, 1976). However, the distinction that Barnes and Shemilt (1974) draw between the different models of learning and teaching that teachers possess is important here. Its full importance is that, in Britton's words (1971) it is in expressive language that 'we are likely to rehearse the growing points of our formulation and analysis of experience.' Bypass the expressive, then, in talk or writing, and it is possible to bypass learning, too.

In reading, the same attention can be paid to process as I have already indicated in discussing talk and writing. Consider reference skills, for instance, which we tend to take for granted: teachers expect their pupils to be able to handle such skills, and complain if they can't. But they are not natural skills and it is not difficult, in any subject, to take the time to introduce pupils of any age to fundamental research procedures of how to use indexes, contents pages and catalogues, how to skim-read for specific information, to follow up bibliographies and keep one's own notes and bibliography. What is more, doing these things as part of the normal curriculum, instead of as isolated 'skills', gives the pupils glimpses of their real purposes, so that there is a vitality about the reference work that is absent when such activities are offered as dissociated exercises. Mary Hoffman (1976) is full of valuable ideas about making reading purposeful.

(9) A biology teacher discovers that her pupils find difficulty in reading the text book in order to précis the main points. She reads a paragraph to them and asks them to tell her what the central point of it was. After discussion, the pupils write down the main idea, and compare their suggestions. The teacher hands out a scientific paper, and tells the students to produce a précis which summarizes its main ideas so that they themselves can use and understand the précis later.

The teacher here has intuitively recognized the weakness of presenting précis as a game with words ('reduce to one third of its length . . .') and has presented it as a function of reading for learning, and as being not about words but about *ideas*.

One of the objections I have heard to the theory of a 'language and learning policy across the curriculum' is that there is nothing new about it. Good teachers, it is said, have always tried to work like this. This is perfectly true. As the team who developed *Breakthrough to Literacy* remarked about their work, there was nothing original about many of the ideas they were describing: they merely synthesized good practice (MacKay *et al.*, 1970). However, this in itself should not be undervalued. A productive synthesis means making available to many more people what was previously confined to a few.

But there is an even more important distinction to be made. There were always good teachers doing inspired work, but they remained isolated within a staff, professionally in touch with, at most, a few colleagues. There were never any channels by which teachers from different subject areas could meet to discuss matters as fundamental as how children learn. What is meant now by 'language across the curriculum' is an opening up of barriers previously closed, and a double sharing by teachers of their insights and perceptions about the business of teaching and learning, in ways that bond colleagues together. There is the sharing first at departmental level, where there are common assumptions about an area of knowledge. Secondly, there is the inter-departmental debate, the true 'language across the curriculum', where teachers of different subjects can meet because they have recognized that what is common to all teachers is the question of how pupils learn best, irrespective of content.

The co-operative discussion begun by teachers trying to explore such questions is constantly supported by testing out and reporting back on different procedures, and by accurate documentation not simply from memory, but by recording on tape what is happening and listening to it afterwards. The constant revaluation of what is happening, the shared ideas and planning leading to a shared approach and policy, are directed towards the central aim of constructing contexts in which pupils can learn and make their learning connect with their own lives. So finally the major question, which ought to be faced squarely by all teachers, is how to relate their subjects to the immediate situations and preoccupations of the pupils, because by doing that the pupils can be led out of these pre-occupations towards seeing the greater, more abstract and generalized relevance to mankind of what we call 'subjects'.

There are many points I have not mentioned that deserve discussion: the fact that most reading in secondary schools occurs in bursts of one minute or less; the fact that although teachers constantly set 'revision' homework, hardly any actually explain what revision is or how to set about it; the assumptions that remain uninspected about what pupils ought to understand, and the shock of discovering what complexity lies behind these assumptions. Should we expect a first-year science class to define 'living' when many educated adults can't? Above all, there is the highly complicated emotion a teacher feels if he allows the pupils to choose their own essay titles and finds they write more efficiently than on set topics; or if he tapes pupils discussing a topic and discovers they get on perfectly well without him. The recognition of these matters begins that shift of orientation that encourages the teacher to become a learner again. His learning this time is not about the subject, but about those processes with which all teachers should be familiar: the ways learning actually operates, and the subtle and complex interconnections between that learning, the pupils' own language, and the public modes of discourse which can be made gradually available to the learners, and which can give so much power over learning.

I am grateful to the following teachers who have allowed me to draw upon their or our combined experience for this essay:

Rick Channing, Janice Drewry, Gill Frith, Ros Gray, John Harwood, Hilary Minns, Sandra Morgan, Edie Parsons.

References

Armstrong, M. (1977) 'Reconstructing knowledge: an example,' In *The Countesthorpe Experience* Watts J., Ed. London: Allen and Unwin.
Barnes, D. (1971) 'Language in the secondary classroom.' In *Language, the Learner and the School* Barnes, D., Britton, J. N. and Rosen, H. Harmondsworth: Penguin Books.
Barnes, D. (1976) *From Communication to Curriculum*. Harmondsworth: Penguin Books.
Barnes, D. and Shemilt, D. (1974) 'Transmission and interpretation,' *Educational Review*, 26, 213–28.

Britton, J. N. (1970) *Language and Learning*. London: Allen Lane, The Penguin Press.

Britton, J. N. (1971) 'What's the use?' *Educational Review, 23*, 205–19.

Britton, J. N., et al. (1975) *The Development of Writing Abilities 11–18*. London: Macmillan.

Des (1975) *A Language for Life* (The Bullock Report). London: HMSO.

Dixon, J. (1974) 'Processes of formulation in group discussion,' *Educational Review, 26*, 241–50.

Hargreaves, D. *et al.* (1975) *Deviance in Classrooms*. London: Routledge.

Hoffman, M. (1976) *Reading, Writing and Relevance*. London: Hodder and Stoughton.

Keddie, N. (1971) 'Classroom knowledge,' in *Knowledge and Control* Young, M. F. D., Ed. London: Collier-Macmillan.

Mackay, D., *et al.* (1970) *Breakthrough to Literacy* (Teachers Manual). London: Longman.

Martin, N., *et al.* (1976) *Writing and Learning Across the Curriculum*. London: Ward Lock Educational.

Nash, R. (1973) *Classrooms Observed*. London: Routledge.

Rosen, H. (1967) 'The language of textbooks,' In Britton, J. N., Ed. *Talking and Writing* London: Methuen.

Rosen, H. (1971) 'Towards a language policy across the curriculum,' In *Language, the Learner and the School* Barnes, D., Britton, J. N. and Rosen, H. Harmondsworth. Penguin Books.

Torbe, M. (1976) *Language Across the Curriculum: Guidelines for Schools*. London: Ward Lock Educational.

8

Second Language Lessons for the Teaching of Reading

ALAN DAVIES

My purpose in this chapter is to examine major developments in reading in second language (L2) teaching and to suggest their implications for the first language (L1) reading teacher. I shall not here make any distinction between second and foreign language teaching; the term L2 will be used to include all kinds of second and foreign language teaching. My concern will be mainly with reading at the advanced level, rather less with intermediate reading and not at all with beginning reading. Among a variety of good work, surveys, reports and essays on L2 reading, the chapters by Rivers (1968) and the paper by Eskey (1973) are excellent summaries. There are indications that L1 teaching of reading is beginning to find linguistics as sharp a stimulus and as useful a tool as does L2. The reviews by Della-Piana and Endo (1973) and by Goodacre (1973) and the perceptive papers by Lunzer (1976) and Reid (1970) are indications that linguistics is soon likely to be more welcome in L1 reading. Indeed, Goodacre points specifically to two areas as of importance to the L1 reading teacher which we shall be discussing below under the heading of the linguistic basis of L2 reading; these are the relation between the spoken and the written languages and the psycholinguistic nature of the reading process.

There are four parts to this chapter. In the first, the major part, I examine the influence of the linguistic view of language on L2 reading, making the assumption that this linguistic view has been of major influence on L2 reading, as on L2 teaching in general. In contrast, the influence on L1 reading, as on L1 teaching, has not been large. Second, I consider practices shared in common between L2 and L1 teaching of reading; third, I ask whether there are lessons L2 practice can learn from L1; I conclude that both theory and practice make it necessary for L1 and L2 curricula to be regarded as aspects of the same activity. They have everything to gain from cooperation.

The linguistic view of L2 reading

To say that L2 reading (more properly, the second language teaching of reading) has a linguistic basis is an exaggeration, just as it is an exaggeration to say that L1 reading has a literary basis. But there is some truth, if only superficial, in both. Undoubtedly L2 and L1 reading have the same aim, which is to achieve meaning from the text. There is, however, a difference, perhaps a major one, in attitude to text. For L1, language is not nearly as important as the meaning that comes through it; for L2, language is very important indeed. The difference in attitude is a very natural one given the different experiences of L2 and L1 readers. Each approach has its advantages and its disadvantages: L2 teaching of reading can be too mechanistic, over-involved in the text and the language structures and never dealing with meaning, but it does also provide procedures, or tries to do so, for coming to terms with the language of the text so that meaning becomes possible. L1, on the other hand, can be too inpressionistic, providing no procedures for understanding the language in order to get at meaning, but it does, quite rightly, stress meaning. This lack of an instructional element in L1, especially for very advanced reading, can cause a frustration which may be glimpsed in the career of I. A. Richards (see Press, 1963) who because he was finding it impractical, early on abandoned his own invention of practical criticism in favour of work on basic language patterns, often for L2 learners.

The focus on language is fundamental to the L2 reading teacher. We shall consider it in terms of four contrasts: the spoken and the written language; text grammars and sentence grammars; learning to read and reading; functional and non-functional reading. My argument will be that an understanding of these four contrasts underlies the best L2 reading practice.

There appear to be major differences in emphasis on spoken and written language between L2 and L1 practice (Abercrombie, 1963). The L1 reader comes to the written medium already knowing the spoken language. The L2 reader may nor may not be able to speak the L2 when he starts. Recent L2 teaching doctrine has maintained that speaking is essential and must normally precede reading (e.g., Derrick, 1966) because speaking is more important practically, and because speech is 'primary', one of the basic tenets (or so it is claimed) of the structural linguists. For the structuralists the spoken language was the 'real' language, and from the linguistic theories stemmed the emphasis on speech that is apparent in the audiolingual methods of language teaching. Reading was not ignored, but it did tend to come later. Current practice, however, has put aside the doctrine of speech before reading. The explosion in L2 teaching (particularly of 'English for Special Purposes' or ESP, mainly for academic purposes) has brought about a change of attitude so that reading frequently develops at the same time and rate as the spoken language, and in some cases only reading (as a 'library language') is taught.

There are several reasons for this change — one is the realization that the spoken and the written languages are formally different; a second is that for many L2 learners the reading skill is what they really need. At the same time as L2 practice has been moving from speaking as primary to reading as equal and perhaps primary, the reverse trend can be discerned in L1 practice where the presumed (but erroneous) rallying cry of linguists that speech is primary has at last been accepted, giving rise to the concept of 'oracy' (Wilkinson, 1974) on the one hand, and providing support to the argument that reading materials should be a linguistic mirror of the spoken language (Goodacre, 1973). This latter effect has been important in L1 teaching and could be far-reaching. Not only is there research into the spoken language element in beginning reading materials (Reid, 1970) and attempts to produce reading materials that are more realistic in terms of the spoken language (Berg, 1969), but there is also condemnation of those reading materials in which the separation of the written from the spoken language is most evident. To condemn in this way seems to me mistaken. Of course some reading materials may be so stilted that they bear no relation to the *written* language, but are entirely artificial. However, criticism tends to be of the 'We never *say* that' rather than 'We never write that' kind.

The effects of the doctrine of the primacy of the spoken language on L1 reading do not end there. There are also sociolinguistic considerations which have to do with more general philosophical and political beliefs about the need to develop and safeguard the child's individual experience and identity with his own background. The effects of this set of beliefs are widespread, in the U.S.A. in the L1 'bidialectalism' debate (Gibson and Levin, 1975) and in the argument over the status of Black English, and, in the U.K., in the controversies over the value of working class and regional dialects. The creative writing movement (Burgess *et al.*, 1973) can be seen as an attempt to make deliberate provision for reading materials that reflect genuine spoken language from real social backgrounds in the most obvious way — by getting children to produce their own.

Such changes in fashion in language teaching are not uncommon. The switch in L2 teaching from speaking to reading as the chief goal is to this writer irritating but understandable. At least in L2 teaching there is recognition that the spoken and the written languages are not mirror images of one another. This is the real linguistic point. It can be argued that the spoken language comes before the written in the life of the individual (the child normally learns to speak before he learns to read) and in the life of the group (there are many examples of languages that are spoken but never written, but no examples of written languages that were never spoken). The spoken language is prior but it is not primary, and in all highly literate communities the written language influences the spoken probably as much as the spoken does the written (Eskey, 1973).

But even if the spoken language were primary as well as being prior, it would still not be the same as the written language. Apart from the differences in terms of elision and reduction, the absence of stress and intonation in written language, its greater formality, there is differential redundancy and there is the difference of the speech event. As regards redundancy the spoken language can, for example, repeat messages, if necessary in the same words. The written language does not necessarily need to repeat, but it does need to make explicit what is only hinted at in the spoken language, for example by providing titles, paragraph headings, and punctuation (see Davies and Widdowson, 1974). At the spoken speech event, both addresser and addressee are present; reading requires only the presence of the addressee. Knowing this, the writer must somehow incorporate into his text those features which, were the interaction spoken, he would present personally (see Widdowson, 1971).

The parallel switch in L1 teaching from reading to speaking is more of a sociolinguistic than a psycholinguistic or an educational demand. What is more, it is a dubious demand (Criper and Davies, 1977). It is that children need to be reassured about the value of their background and origins, represented in this case by the spoken language. It is for just this reason, I suggest, that Black English has enjoyed a vogue in the States, as has working class English in this country. For the same reason there is growing interest in bilingualism-bidialectalism in the United States, which implies the preservation in all children of the home dialect or language by according it prestige and by teaching in it for the first few years. Now it may be true that it is the job of the school to reassure children about their homes and family backgrounds and home languages or dialects. That is arguable. But the written language should not always reflect the spoken language; they are sometimes two realizations of the same code, and sometimes they are two different codes. To suggest to the child that there is no difference is to deceive him and misrepresent both the spoken and the written languages.

L2 teaching also distinguishes between sentence grammar — largely concerned with linguistic categories such as nouns and verbs — and text grammar, which involves logical-rhetorical categories such as conjunction and reference. This distinction is more characteristic of written than of spoken language. The development of materials for learning English for academic purposes (Lackstrom *et al.*, 1970; Kaplan, 1972; Urquhart, 1977; Allen and Widdowson, 1974) has given a boost to the application of discourse theory. Interest in logical-rhetorical relations, in speech acts and functions (Halliday, 1973) and in establishing categories for cohesion and coherence (Halliday and Hasan, 1976) has also developed: most practical expression has been in the delineation of notional syllabuses (Wilkins, 1976). While stressing the grammar of texts, L2 teaching has not lost sight of the need of learners to acquire the grammar of the written sentence. There is some disagreement on whether attention to sentence grammar has any value at all and in particular whether a concentration on 'mere' linguistic competence (i.e., the internalizing of sentence grammars) will ensure the acquisition of the wider communicative competence (Paulson and Bruder, 1976). However, there does seem to be general agreement that some linguistic competence is a prerequisite to communicative competence. Now, in reading, communicative competence means the ability to understand for example, implication, denial, and suggestion, as well as to make judgements of appropriate language use. But the important point to make here is that the L2 reader already has a good deal of L2 reading practice at the sentence level. Given that it is acceptable to use such non-authentic texts as single sentences for reading practice, I reckon that the gap between sentence and text has been lessened as a result of work on discourse, since both sentence and text depend upon discourse organization for their understanding. Attempts have been made to make available this work on discourse in study texts (Candlin, *et al.*, 1974; Urquhart, 1977).

The L1 reading situation is less satisfactory. The anti-grammar movement has not helped with learning of the grammar of the sentence and in spite of the emphasis Goodman (1967) puts on following a line of argument, an ability he subdivides into cognitive styles, there does not seem to be help available for L1 readers in handling the text grammar. And yet this is just where Smith (1971), Goodman (1967), Cooper and Petrosky (1976), all of whom emphasize prediction in reading, insist we should be operating. The problem is to know how to do so, for both teacher and student. The Goodman model of reading as a psycholinguistic guessing game has been widely accepted. It is not clear how this guessing works or how it can be facilitated (Eskey, 1973). Indeed, guessing seems a curious term to use since it suggests randomness, which is an unsatisfactory account of L1 fluent reading and an unhelpful hint to the learner. L2 teaching, which draws on sociolinguistics, offer a range of concerns over discourse.

L2 teaching of reading also makes a clear distinction between reading and learning to read. Smith (1971) does offer an explanation of the way guessing works. This is his 'reduction of uncertainty', as the individual brings his own experience to bear on the text. He suggests that when we read, we check up on the knowledge and conceptual organization we bring to a text. Thus the sentence, 'Lloyd George was a great orator' has meaning only if we know the linguistic class memberships and the concept references. But it is not clear whether the knowledge we bring is of the parts or of the whole; do we bring to the sentence quoted above a knowledge of the parts and come away with a sense of the whole; i.e., that it is Lloyd George who is the orator, that as an orator he is great, that this is an opinion that might have been in question, and so on? Or do we bring to the sentence all this knowledge and then come away having confirmed what we knew already? Either meaning seems possible in terms of the prediction theories, but the force of Smith's argument does suggest that it is the second version which is intended, that is, that the purpose of reading is to confirm existing knowledge. This view of reading is deeply pessimistic: its logical extreme is that we cannot learn to read anything which we do not already know. In other words, we simply cannot learn to read.

Smith is characterizing efficient or fluent reading and doing so from a psychological point of view. But the efficient reader's strategies do not , by definition, require assistance; at issue is just how to become efficient. No doubt the achievement of efficient reading involves learning how to apply one's previous knowledge to a text, but it is unclear how this is done; nor is it clear to the learner reader how he is to crack the linguistic code of the text itself, a code that has a structure of its own, independent of who is reading it and which kind of knowledge and experience he brings with him.

In the L2 reading situation the need for cracking the linguistic code is clear. The reader, normally, does not speak the L2 as a native and for him there must be emphasis, as a reader, on the language. This is not the case in practice for the L1 reader who, it is assumed, does know the code. Concentration for him therefore can afford to be on the extra-linguistic features, on the referential and implicational features of the text and on himself as a reader. For the completely fluent L1 reader this is fine, but for the non-fluent reader, that is, a learner, or the inadequate reader, that is a subnormal one, this is not satisfactory since what he needs is language instruction. Here, with its wealth of exercise and practice and graded material L2 teaching has something to offer L1 teaching (Mackay, 1976; Wilson, 1973; Pierce, 1975; Berman, 1975). It is interesting to note a change here in directional influence. Twenty years ago L1 practice was influencing L2, perhaps because so many L2 teachers were by training and perhaps sympathy L1 teachers, so that it was possible to say to an L2 class, 'you learn to read by reading' — an excessively unhelpful remark. Today there is much less L1 influence on L2 practice because so many young teachers now go straight into L2 teaching. But this is also because L1 teaching has not yet accepted its *language* teaching role.

The L2 teaching profession has found it difficult to accept that language is functional. This applies directly to reading, since in the area of academic purposes it is above all reading that is functional. And within reading, among all possible texts and possible organizations of text, there are samples that are more appropriate for some purposes than for others. Hence the build-up in recent years of English for Special Purposes, with particular selections being made from and instruction given in the English of, for example, workshop practice (Mountford, 1975), mechanical engineering (Glendinning, 1974) and special attention given to English for industry (Jupp, 1975). It is not clear just what the linguistic distinctions between one kind of English and another are, though it is generally accepted that there are differences, perhaps only of a surface and trivial kind. The reason for mentioning such efforts is to illustrate the acceptance of function, of use for a purpose, usually vocational, in L2 teaching.

This acceptance of function has simply not been made so overwhelmingly in L1 teaching, with the result that the only materials available for adult literacy tuition have in the past been either children's remedial books or L2 texts and exercises. It is fortunate, therefore, that so far nowhere near the two million potential illiterates have come forward in the U.K. for tuition. Perhaps the figures are wrong. If they are right then perhaps the mass of those at risk have no need of literacy — which is in itself a kind of functional definition of literacy. As Ray (1968) says of language planning, we shall get nowhere by need creating. The acquisition of literacy or of language has to fulfil an existing need. Need creating is not viable. An individual who reaches adulthood without literacy has probably come to terms with his state to such an extent that he has no 'need' for literacy. All his habits, his whole life style are based on illiteracy. He passes for literate when he must, but most of the time he does not need to be literate. The only way to break his inadequacy is to ensure that his new literacy fits into the world of subterfuge and non-script that he daily inhabits, in such a way as to help him continue with his existing habits. Once literacy becomes a habit for him it will then become a catalyst in his life, but it cannot be that at first.

Common L2 and L1 practices

So far I have suggested four areas in which the view of language shared by many L2 teachers seems to be of relevance to L1 practice. All four discussions indicate that L2 teachers view language (linguistically defined) as central to their concerns. It is likely that L1 teachers for whom language is merely a filter or code that transmits meaning do not share this view. Thus the ideal L2 reading class consists of texts and related materials, the effect of which is to bring the students back, always back, to the language of the texts (Harris, 1966). My impression is that generally there is no such return in the L1 class, where the purpose of the text is to provide a stimulus for discussion, argument and opinion. In other words the L2 learner is regarded as a *language* learner and the L1 learner usually is not.

The importance of language for the L2 learner has implications for the content and the method of his reading instruction. Consider, first, the more general area of the techniques of L2 language instruction (which include reading, of course). Language laboratory work, programmed instruction, error analysis, syllabus planning, pedagogic grammar, vocabulary exercises all show that L2 teaching deals directly with language and attempts to analyse it for the learner in a way that makes sense of the language. One approach to the organization of a course of language instruction is to follow the stages of methodics (Mackey, 1965): selection, grading and presentation of the language materials. Another way takes us directly into the narrower reading field, and that is simplification. Simplification is the pedagogic method *par excellence*; lectures, teacher explanations, textbook descriptions, scientific magazines all provide a simpler (which may be also longer) account of the material. Simplification in education is no more than making a message available to an audience other than the one for whom it was first intended. Hence in L2 reading materials, the great spate of 'simplified versions' is often of literary material though some technical material is included. It is interesting that the literary simplifications tend to derive from traditional originals: *Oliver Twist, The Mill on the Floss, Gulliver's Travels*. But there are good reasons for this concentration on great books and for the absence of specially written simpler material. The reasons are, first, that the special material, desirable though it may be, is difficult to create, and, second, that the strength of the traditional plot and character endure through the reduction of linguistic difficulty (see Davies, 1974).

It is interesting to compare the parallel series of readers produced for L1 readers, for example the 'Tales Retold for Easy Reading' in which the simplification technique is similar to that in the L2 reading materials in terms of syntax but with inevitably less emphasis on vocabulary selection, the (probably correct) assumption being that L1 readers can tolerate a wider variety of vocabulary load than can L2 readers of similar educational level. Notice that the L1 reading materials are typically intended for remedial or adjustment classes; that is, they are not considered to be of value (as are the L2 reading materials) for normal children or students.

What are the techniques used for L2 simplification? First, let us dispose of a measuring technique that has *not* been widely used. This is the readability index, which purports to measure the absolute readability, that is, the ease or difficulty of a text (Gilliland, 1972). This index has had some influence on L1 practice, little effect on L2. Why this is so is not clear, since the actual techniques used by L2 simplifiers are not refined ones (see Davies and Widdowson, 1974). They are first, the vocabulary count (e.g., Thorndike and Lorge, 1944; West, 1953) which is used deliberately to restrict the level of new or uncommon words used in a series of texts. There are serious criticisms against this use of vocabulary counts, in particular that common words are not necessarily easier than uncommon ones. After all, the functional load of a common homonym (e.g., *match, get*) is such that its meaning may be conveyed totally by context — which means that the reader who does not understand the context will have no way of deciding which of the meanings of the word to select. Second, after the use of a vocabulary word-list some attention is paid to the syntax and to the situational or content features of the text. The situations are reduced; characters, places and times are curtailed. The syntax is teased out in such a way as to make explicit the underlying syntactic relations; thus compound sentences become simple ones, inversions are restored, transformations brought back to the canonical form. There is method in simplifying, though it is not clear how explicit it is to the simplifier.

All L2 teaching materials, whether given the name nor not, are simplifications — which is another way of saying that all language samples, in grammars as much as in teaching materials, are forms of idealization. L2 teaching necessarily selects and grades (or places in sequence) its materials against some yardstick of difficulty. It is instructive to observe the present debate in the L2 teaching profession over just what that yardstick should be; in the past it has normally been grammatical, though it has always been admitted that there is no final way of saying that one grammatical form is more difficult than another; recently there has been the interest in functions, in notional syllabuses and in communicative competence and as a result some attempt (Van Ek, 1975) to use a functional rather than a formal (i.e., grammatical) grading. This has proved very difficult, and it now looks as though it will still be necessary, even with a functional or notional syllabus in mind, to make use of the underlying grammatical framework for grading purposes. L2 teachers certainly expect materials in *Course Book 1* to be easier than those in *Book 2*, in terms of language; and they expect that the lessons or units within *Course Book 1* will also progress in terms of difficulty. As I have noted, it is not easy to spell out just what *easy* and *difficult* mean here, since there is no final way of saying that, for example, the present simple tense in English is easier than the past continuous.

All L2 teaching materials, then — texts, exercises on texts and so on — are simplifications in that they attempt to provide the learner with successive approximations (Corder, 1974) to the target language. How they do this is, as I have said, unclear. They seem to change the surface structure of a text back into its deep structure so that, for example, ambiguity, which is a surface structure phenomenon, is removed. Now the effect of this, as with all language manipulation, is to draw attention to the language or the expression at the expense of the meaning or the content. That is to say that, while an attempt is certainly made to retain the message of the text, inevitably the language changes cause some distortion. Or do they? If the language is changed is the meaning changed? This is really a question about our view on linguistic relativity. Perhaps the sensible answer is that at the more stylistic/literary end of a scale, for example, in poetry, there is a change of meaning and that at the other end, for example, in a government report, the same message may be conveyed in many ways, some easier than others. When an explainer — who may be a teacher — says, 'Let me put it another way' or 'Let me put it in other words,' he believes that it is possible to send the same message in other, simpler, language. (Translation is a special case of simplifying, in which differences of cultural background must make some messages very difficult to translate).

Readability measures have, as has been mentioned, been used in L1 teaching but have recently been superseded by the cloze procedure, a device which Bormuth (1969) and others, following Taylor (1953), developed. Cloze has become popular in L1 practice, more perhaps as a category of reading exercise than as either a readability measure or as a comprehension measure. In L2 practice, cloze has also become very popular, but is used mainly as a test format (Oller, 1971). It is unfortunate but understandable that L1 teaching should seize on cloze as a reading exercise format: superficially it looks like a helpful *language* exercise — precisely what I have said L1 teaching needs — but in fact it remains quite mysterious; since, as in poetry, there is no way of knowing just why one word rather than another should be inserted, there is no appropriate way for the teacher to provide helpful instruction; it is a psycholinguistic guessing game.

The increasing interest in L2 teaching seems to represent a growing unease with the structuralist tradition of taxonomic materials, a feeling that language should not be broken down into its component parts, since it is not a machine, and we do not know what the parts really are. The integrative test, such as cloze, which does not pretend to analyse, is therefore very appealing. It is, of course, seductively dangerous, since its deliberate lack of precision can give it an untestable certainty. In L2 teaching cloze has moved from a narrow to a much more general use: from a readability measure through comprehension testing to general language proficiency testing. The very reliability of cloze testing can be an argument used to outweigh its vague validity. If an L2 test claims to test the whole of the language (as is now claimed for cloze; see Oller, 1971) in what sense can we query the validity of the test, what criterion is there for a global measure?

Naturally, with the pedagogic stress on and interest in incremental learning, L2 teaching has made much use of tests, and has as a result accumulated a good deal of expertise in this area. In L2 testing cloze has become a powerful technique, but the more traditional discrete point or separate skill tests are still much used. The nature and extent of L2 teaching demand an apparatus of testing that does not belong in a situation in which the language is already known, as in L1 teaching. For the L1 learner, reading is as much an acquired or superposed code as is L2; they are both acquired systems. Teachers of L2, and of L1 reading, make use of reading comprehension tests and multiple choice items. And these are transferred, quite properly, from tests into exercises, as with the Science Research Associates reading materials. A test for a less advanced group is an exercise for a more advanced one. Testing at its most useful in L2 teaching also throws the concern and the effort back on the content of the teaching, through attempts to devise diagnostic tests that will seek out suitable remedies and through criterion referenced tests that do seem to demand a judicious analysis of levels of appropriate attainment in an area. The difficulty with both cloze and criterion referencing is that they tend to be publicized with missionary zeal. But this is the L2 teaching plague. L2 teaching needs a stability that is not rocked as fashions change; cloze and criterion referenced testing need to be added to the techniques and approaches already used, not become the only ones. A similar warning is probably necessary for the teaching of L1 reading, also susceptible to fashion.

L1 lessons for L2

I have mentioned some of the linguistic views taken in L2 teaching and noted some of its current practices, both areas of interest to the L1 teacher. Now I want to mention some aspects of current L1 practice and this time ask what value these have for the L2 teacher. I will mention four — spoken English, reading materials, content analysis and the teaching of literature. In all four areas L1 English practice is excellent; it is interesting to speculate why this is so. It may be that when L1 does accept certain learning problems as linguistic ones, L1 teachers can rely on an understanding in the learner that can be assumed only in the L1.

So in the spoken language area a great deal of good creative work has been done on 'oracy' (Wilkinson, 1974) which has raised the level of the discussion to ask creatively just what ranges and skills should we expect in the spoken language, not only just what can we test (which tends to be the L2 position). In reading materials the SRA are the best of their kind (there is nothing comparable in L2 teaching of reading), again because they assume a linguistic sophistication that cannot exist among L2 learners. They have a serious flaw, it is true, in that they do not show the reader where he has gone wrong. There is no diagnosis, no instruction. The reader knows only that he has failed or succeeded, not why or how he has done either. If he suceeds this may not matter, but it certainly does if he fails, since only by knowing why and how he erred can the reader improve.

The third area is a kind of content analysis, an attempt not yet (as far as I know) matched in L2 teaching, which studies bias in texts, a bias presumably brought about by the choice of language. The Open University Reading Courses (Davies, 1974; Zimet, 1977) provide some discussion here.

The fourth area is that of literature teaching in which the teacher frequently puts the onus of judgement and interpretation back on to the readers. When he has good students this makes excellent sense. But when, as in many classrooms, the majority of students are average, then they need some support. Again, of course, literature teaching can succeed because of what can be assumed about knowledge and understanding of the language. The same point was made in connection with both oracy and the SRA materials.

What this means, then, is that the L2 and L1 learners have quite different strengths. The L2 learner can fall back on his own mother tongue, his L1, in order to understand content, discuss a meaning, or parallel a linguistic difficulty. In the L1 case there is no other L1 to fall back on. But as the learner develops in language and in experience, then it becomes possible to make assumptions about both his language range and his knowledge of the world. So for advanced readers Smith (1971) is right; we agreed on this earlier.

On the whole, L2 teaching is more mechanistic but works towards the affective, though it may be a functional affect. L1 teaching takes the mechanistic realm for granted and is concerned wholly with the affective. L2 teaching may set its sights too low, L1 teaching frequently sets its too high. Each must learn from the other.

The L1 – L2 Continuum

Educationally and psychologically a language may be superposed, just as a dialect can be; for example, standard English is learned by speakers of another, less prestigious dialect in, say, South Wales or Newfoundland. This is paralleled by the superposing of Standard English on the native French speaking child in Quebec or Welsh speaking child in Wales. We may control a range of dialects, some of which may be given the names of languages. Linguistically, language and dialect cannot be distinguished: for example, some of the southern dialects of German, in Bavaria, say, are quite as different from Standard High German as is Dutch, and yet they are called dialects while Dutch is called a language. Socially, a switch from one dialect to another (for reasons of, say, change of situation, addressee, topic, etc.) carries the same meaning as a move from one language to another. A further parallel is that languages are distinguished from one another in terms of prestige in certain settings (e.g., in a colonial situation) just as much as dialects can be. It is convenient, therefore, to regard bilingualism and bidialectalism as a continuum on which we can all be placed, since we are all bidialectals and many of us are bilinguals. Now if bidialectalism is in fact a special case of bilingualism, and it is my argument that it is, then what L1 teaching has to learn above all from L2 teaching is that code learning cannot be taken for granted — it needs to be taught; and that instruction in the language and in reading a text as an exemplar of all other texts, is essential. L2 and L1 learners are both language learners. Reading first of all involves language, and it is important that the emphasis in reading for L1 teaching should be where it clearly is in the best L2 practice — on language.

References

Abercrombie, D. (1963) 'Conversation and spoken prose,' *English Language Teaching, 18*, 10–16.

Allen, J. P. B. and Widdowson, H. G. (1974) 'Teaching the communicative use of English,' *International Review of Applied Linguistics, 12*.

Berg, L., Ed. (1969) *Nippers* (groups of graded books for children, aged 6–9). Basingstoke: Macmillan.

Berman, R. (1975) 'An analytic syntax: a technique for advanced level reading,' *TESOL Quarterly, 9*, 243–51.

Bormuth, J. R. (1969) 'Factor validity of cloze tests as measures of reading comprehension ability,' *Reading Research Quarterly, 4*, 358–65.

Burgess, C., et al. (1973) *Understanding Children Writing*. Harmondsworth: Penguin Books.

Candlin, C., Kirkwood, J. M. and Moore, H. N. (1974) *Study Skills in English*. Department of English, Lancaster University.

Cooper, C. R. and Petrosky, A. R. (1976) 'A psycholinguistic view of the reading process,' *Journal of Reading, 20*, 184–207.

Corder, S. P. (1974) 'Error analysis, interlanguage and second language acquisition,' In *Error Analysis: Perspectives on Second Language Acquisition* Richards, J. C., Ed. London: Longman.

Criper, C. and Davies, A., (1977) 'Research on spoken language in the Primary School,' In *Language and Learning in Early Childhood* Davies, A., Ed. London: Heinemann.

Davies, A. and Widdowson, H. G. (1974) 'Reading and writing,' In *Techniques in Applied Linguistics* Allen, J. P B. and Corder, S. P., Eds. (Vol. 3 of Edinburgh Course in Applied Linguistics). London: Oxford University Press.

Davies, A. (1974) *Printed Media and the Reader.* (PE 261, Reading Development, Units 8 and 9). Milton Keynes: The Open University Press.

Della-Piana, G. M. and Endo, G. T. (1973) 'Reading research,' In *Second Handbook of Research on Teaching* Travers, R. M. W., Ed. Chicago: Rand McNally.

Derrick, J. (1966) *Teaching English to Immigrants.* London: Longman.

Eskey, D. E. (1973) 'A model program for teaching advanced reading to students of English as a foreign language,' *Language Learning, 23,* 169–84.

Gilliland, J. (1972) *Readability.* London: University of London Press.

Glendinning, E. H. (1974). *English in Mechanical Engineering.* London: Oxford University Press.

Gibson, E. J. and Levin, E. H. (1975) *The Psychology of Reading.* Cambridge, Mass.: The MIT Press.

Goodacre, E. (1973) 'Reading,' In *Educational Research in Britain, 3,* Butcher, H. J. and Pont, H. B., Eds. London: University of London Press.

Goodman, K. S. (1967) 'Reading: a psycholinguistic guessing game,' *Journal of the Reading Specialist, 6,* 126–35.

Halliday, M. A. K. (1973) *Explorations in the Functions of Language.* London: Edward Arnold.

Halliday, M. A. K. and Hasan, R. (1976) *Cohesion in English.* London: Longman.

Harris, D. P. (1966) *Reading Improvement Exercises for Students of English as a Second Language.* Englewood Cliffs, New Jersey: Prentice-Hall.

Jupp, T. C. and Hodlin, S. (1975) *Industrial English: An Example of Theory and Practice in Functional Language Teaching.* London: Heinemann.

Kaplan, R. B. (1972) *The Anatomy of Rhetoric.* Philadelphia: Center for Curriculum Development.

Lackstrom, J. E., Selinker, L. and Trimble, L. P. (1970). 'Grammar and technical English,' In *English as a Second Language: Current Issues* Lugton, R. C., Ed. Philadelphia: Center for Curriculum Development.

Lunzer, E. A. (1975). 'Schools Council Project: The Effective Use of Reading,' In *The Content of Reading* Cashdan, A., Ed. London: Ward Lock Educational.

Mackay, R. and Mountford, A. (1976). 'Teaching reading for information,' In *Reading: Insights and Approaches* Anthony, E. and Richards, J., Eds. Singapore: Singapore University Press.

Mackey, W. F. (1965) *Language Teaching Analysis.* London: Longman.

Mountford, A. (1975) *English in Workshop Practice.* London: Oxford University Press.

Oller, J. W. and Conrad, C. A. (1971) 'The cloze technique and ESL proficiency,' *Language Learning, 21,* 183–95.

Paulson, C. B. and Bruder, M. B. (1976) *Teaching English as a Second Language: Techniques and Procedures.* Cambridge, Mass.: Withrop.

Pierce, M. E. (1975) 'Teaching the use of formal redundancy in reading for ideas,' *TESOL Quarterly, 9,* 253–70.

Press, J., Ed. (1963) *The Teaching of English Literature Overseas.* London: Methuen.

Ray, P. S. (1968) 'Language Standardization,' In *Readings in the Sociology of Language* Fishman, J. A., Ed. The Hague: Mouton.

Reid, J. F. (1970) 'Sentence structure in reading primers,' *Research in Education, 3,* 23–37.

Rivers, W. (1968) *Teaching Foreign Language Skills.* Chicago: University of Chicago Press.

Smith, F. (1971) *Understanding Reading.* New York: Holt, Rinehart and Winston.

Taylor, W. L. (1953) 'Cloze procedure: a new tool for measuring readability,' *Journalism Quarterly, 30,* 415–33.

Thorndike, E. L. and Lorge, I. (1944) *The Teacher's Wordbook of 30,000 Words.* New York: Teachers' College, University of Columbia.

Urquhart, A. H. (1977) *The Effect of Rhetorical Organisation on the Readability of Study Texts.* PhD thesis, University of Edinburgh.

Van Ek, J. A. (1975) *The Threshold Level.* Strasbourg: Council of Europe.

West, M., Ed. (1953) *A General Service List of English Words, with Semantic Frequencies and a Supplementary Wordlist for the Writing of Popular Science and Technology.* London: Longman.

Widdowson, H. G. (1971) 'The teaching of rhetoric to students of science and technology', In *Science and Technology in a Second Language.* London: CILT.

Wilkins, D. A. (1976) *National Syllabuses.* London: Oxford University Press.

Wilkinson, A., Stratta, L. and Dudley, P. (1974) *The Quality of Listening.* London: Macmillan (for the Schools Council).

Wilson, L. I. (1973) 'Reading in the ESOL Classroom: a Technique for Teaching Syntactic Meaning,' *TESOL Quarterly, 7,* 259–67.

Zimet, S. G. (1977) *Printed Media and the Reader.* (PE 231, Reading Development, Units 9 and 10). Milton Keynes: The Open University Press.

9
Standards
and
Assessment

DENIS VINCENT

Until recently, assessment has been very much a poor relation in the teaching of reading and other language skills. The quality of published test materials is often outshone by that of the schemes, materials and teaching techniques which have been created. In the classroom, teachers have often been content to base their evaluations of standards and progress on archaic or technically primitive methods, as surveys of testing practice have shown (DES, 1975; Nicholls, 1975).

The main purpose of this chapter is, therefore, to examine a small selection of the assessment issues that are relevant to the teaching of reading and to consider some of the problems and possibilities associated with them.

The first section deals with some of the ramifications of the national monitoring programme recommended in the Bullock Report (DES, 1975). This is an operation that is seemingly remote from work in individual schools or classrooms, but the discussion centres upon the extent to which it might eventually influence assessment at a practical level. The second section deals with the problems associated with measuring 'comprehension', as this is a problem in dire need of clarification, both for national survey purposes and testing in schools. For similar reasons the third section deals with the measurement of spelling. Finally, some thought is given to the general improvement of assessment techniques in school and the form it might take.

NATIONAL STANDARDS

Since the early 1970s, there has been an extensive debate over the question of whether British national standards of reading were in decline, as a National Foundation of Educational Research (NFER) survey (Start and Wells, 1972) had appeared to show. Conclusions on this must be circumscribed by the now widely-held view that the methods that had been employed to measure national standards were unsatisfactory. This resulted in a number of firm recommendations in Bullock on methods and procedures to be adopted for monitoring standards in the future.

Admittedly, Bullock's sections on standards and monitoring are those to which the teacher of reading is least likely to turn, as they deal with a national debate, rather than with practical issues at school or classroom level. Nevertheless, these recommendations are among the few in the report that have received official financial support for their implementation. It is therefore pertinent to consider what general implications they may have for the teaching of reading.

The monitoring procedure would involve a system of long-term evaluation of the reading and writing skills of eleven- and fifteen-year-olds. A bank or pool of tests and assessment materials, designed to cover a wide range of reading and writing skills, would be established. Testing would be carried out by a team of researchers who would conduct a series of surveys each year. These might involve relatively small numbers of pupils at any one time — 'light samples' — but cumulatively they would permit a picture of national trends and progress to be built up.

Some of the main virtues of the proposed system are only incidental to the teaching of reading, but the intention that in future national assessment of reading and writing should be wide-ranging in its coverage of language skills is of central importance. By taking account of the breadth and diversity of behaviours subsumed under the terms 'reading' and 'writing', the monitoring exercise could act as a nationally-based diagnosis of these skills. Surveys carried out in this way might demonstrate not only whether overall standards had changed, but in what particular respects this was so — a way of expressing results that could convey a constructive message for teaching.

Criterion-referenced measures

The adoption of a question-bank, rather than a single test for monitoring could also have far-reaching consequences. In particular, it might give considerable impetus to the development of 'criterion-referenced' tests.

The basic principle of criterion-referenced assessment is that a test or question should measure whether a pupil has or has not mastered a specified skill, or reached a certain level of competence. A criterion-referenced test thus seeks to measure what has been learned, rather than how much better or worse than average a pupil happens to be. In a few areas of reading, notably the testing of phonics, rudimentary criterion-referenced measures have existed for some time. In many other important areas, however, such as the higher order comprehension skills, very little satisfactory work has yet been done. As the monitoring surveys are to involve readers at ages eleven and fifteen, it seems likely that some thought will be given to the more advanced reading skills, and teaching at this level would certainly benefit considerably if teachers had the means to obtain more information about a pupil's strengths and weaknesses.

The Schools Council Effective Use of Reading Project (Lunzer and Gardner, 1977), for example, noted the difficulty many secondary school pupils encountered in meeting the reading demands of project/topic work. It seems likely that teachers would be greatly assisted in fostering the skills necessary to carry out such project work in the spirit intended, if initially they were equipped with tools for measuring the requisite skills. In such an area of the curriculum, where the teacher is concerned with readers' capacity to meet the demands of the immediate situation, rather than with their standing relative to one another or to an external 'norm', criterion-referenced measures are by far the most suitable.

Question banks

There are still considerable problems to be solved in the identification and measurement of skills such as those referred to. It seems likely, though, that in the immediate future the source for real progress in this field will be the development work necessary for the setting up and maintaining of question-banks for national monitoring. It should be stressed that the benefits will be largely indirect; teachers could not expect to have access to the materials to be used in the monitoring exercise itself, at least initially. However, the pioneering experience gained in the development of materials for the bank would make the subsequent development of materials for use by teachers a much more routine exercise than it would be otherwise. Further, once a bank was established and operational, it could provide a base or reference point for the development of separate 'open' banks. Thus, open materials intended for classroom use could be developed alongside, or out of, those restricted for monitoring purposes. The calibration methods that can be employed in question-banking (see Willmott and Fowler, 1974) would also make it possible to render any open materials just as statistically authoritative as closed ones. Indeed, the development of test-materials need not necessarily remain the prerogative of the researchers who operate the bank. A group of teachers wishing to develop tests in an area of special interest to themselves could do so by administering their own tests locally, together with materials of known statistical properties which had been drawn from the central bank. The results for the new materials could be related to the existing data for the bank materials, thus 'standardizing' the new materials.

The foregoing is intended as an illustration of the possibilities inherent in the proposed national monitoring system, not an account of outcomes that can be firmly expected to materialize. Similarly, the statistical item-analysis procedures that would allow for flexible use and further development of such tests are not the only means of constructing a question bank. Nevertheless, a monitoring procedure that revolves around a bank of questions, rather than a single test, inevitably draws the attention of the test-developer towards what each test-task or category of test-task is measuring, as do some of the statistical techniques that could be employed. The monitoring proposals thus create opportunities for innovation and development which might ultimately benefit teachers concerned with the assessment of reading skill.

Definition of literacy

A further, and perhaps more specific, outcome of the monitoring procedure, related to the criterion-reference issue, would be the development of clearer definitions of 'literacy' itself. The debate about standards of literacy has for a long time been obscured by the ambiguity of the term 'literacy'. Different interest groups have used the term to mean different things, though each has tended to speak of literacy as if it were a single absolute state.

At the present time, in spite of the extent of public debate about literacy, there are no truly operational definitions of literacy that might be treated as goals for literacy teaching or as criteria for identifying a person as 'literate'. The dilemma of the teacher is illustrated by the fact that in the aftermath of the 1970/71 NFER Survey (Start and Wells, 1972), a number of head teachers requested copies of the special survey test, NS6, to find out whether pupils in their particular schools reflected the alleged decline in reading standards. It is sad to think that at the time there were no more concrete or practical means by which this might have been done.

The criteria that have been applied to the measurement of literacy in the past are unlikely to be of much service in the future. Social, economic and educational historians, for example, have been able to use the ability to sign one's own name as a sign of literacy, largely because in previous centuries it could be taken as indicative of having attained a substantial degree of reading proficiency (see Schofield, 1968), an assumption that can no longer be made. National surveys in this century have taken the average levels of attainment test performance of seven- and nine-year-old readers as denoting the boundaries of illiteracy and semi-literacy. These criteria sufficed in an era that required quick and cheap measures of progress in literacy, but it is no longer possible to think of literacy in the limited and simplistic form represented by Watts–Vernon and NS6 survey tests, nor, if overall standards change with time, do normative age-related criteria provide an unequivocal yardstick, as the report of the 1970/71 survey shows.

Indeed, norms based on the average test scores of particular age groups cannot be regarded as acceptable criteria by which schools can judge an individual pupil's literacy. It has been standard practice for teachers to treat a child's reading attainment as satisfactory if his chronological age and reading scores match, or the latter exceeds the former. This practice involves the questionable assumption that what the average reader can do is necessarily or automatically sufficient and adequate. There is a growing feeling among reading specialists that the 'average' reader is often not equal to the reading requirements of his education or of everyday life. Such thinking certainly influenced the Bullock Committee, who cited a research study that dramatizes the point (Bormuth, 1969) and concluded that standards 'can and should be raised'. In all, we cannot assume that what an average or typical reader can probably do at eleven or fifteen years is necessarily enough. In any case, we have yet to establish empirically what it is this average reader is really capable of doing. If only for this reason, criterion-referenced tests of literacy seem desirable.

It would be premature to speculate upon the exact form or content of the definition of literacy that will arise out of the national monitoring programme. The very virtue of the proposed scheme is that it creates an opportunity for more careful prior thought and research than has been possible before.

A number of possible guidelines for this exercise already exist. The Open University's Post Experience Courses in Reading Development, for example, require students to give systematic consideration to the reading demands of everyday life. Bormuth (1973) has discussed in some detail 'parameters' that must be taken into consideration if we are to formulate scientific rather than intuitive definitions of literacy. He argues that these must include our present knowledge about the nature of the reading process, the economic and educational consequences of equating any given criterion of test performance with literacy, the linguistic contexts in which the reader is expected to be competent, and the limits imposed by his abilities and aspirations. The procedures Bormuth describes for the implementation of literacy tests based on these considerations appear too speculative for practical use, but his general rationale for defining literacy is one that deserves serious attention. It presents factors that can hardly be ignored if real improvements in the way literacy is defined are to be made.

Implications for schools

Given that it proves possible to produce tests that measure the levels of language attainment necessary for, say, successful functioning in school at the start of secondary education and successful functioning in daily life at the end of compulsory schooling, a question arises as to the impact of such tests.

In the first place, the use of light sampling techniques and the confidential status of the tests would tend to reduce backwash effects or over-specific coaching of pupils on any particular test-task. However, if the tests do embody operational definitions of literacy of a type in advance of any that have gone before, or indeed if they are to be used as evidence on the question of national standards, it would be undesirable to observe complete secrecy about their contents indefinitely. Certainly, it would be awkward to make criticisms or point out areas of weakness without close reference to the methods used for observing weaknesses; how else could teachers be equipped to evaluate their own subsequent efforts to remedy the shortcomings?

It is thus by no means perverse to regard the monitoring of tests as beneficial, especially if it proves possible to make them criterion-referenced. Ideally, they would provide a statement in specific and directly observable terms of the behaviours that constitute literacy. As such, they would not only let teachers know how far short of a satisfactory level of literacy their pupils were; they would also provide constructive guidance for working towards the literacy goal. This is undeniably a somewhat prescriptive use of testing, but then so is any truly diagnostic form of assessment. The criterion-referenced test, by definition, measures actual behaviours we wish the learner to acquire. In the foregoing, the emphasis has been placed deliberately upon the positive role the national monitoring programme could play, for there is no shortage of critics for this, as for any other testing enterprise. Two points of criticism should however be discussed here.

Tests and the curriculum

It is possible that in seeking to produce tighter and measurable definitions of literacy the survey will be seen as an unwarranted intrusion upon the curriculum. Given that the definitions produced are carefully thought out and, as far as possible, empirically-validated, such rejection will surely come only from those who think that literacy teaching is really not their responsibility in the first place. The fundamental development work done for the programme could assist both in clarifying and illuminating the general debate about the nature of literacy and in providing individual teachers with a stimulus for sharpening their own thinking and teaching; it would be a pity if all this were rejected on principle.

Validity

Criterion-referenced tests are being produced in the U.S.A. in ever-increasing quantities, and the innovatory work which might be undertaken by British researchers producing survey materials could be redundant. But these objections can be answered in the following ways. First, the tests that already exist are very often components in highly structured published teaching programmes and the behaviours they purport to measure are so specific to these programmes as to seem trivial in a more general assessment of literacy. Second, the validity of these tests is often highly questionable, as a study by Macfarlane (1976) has demonstrated. The research work which might precede the surveys could usefully concentrate upon the identification of the more salient aspects of literacy and upon valid means of assessing them. This would be a difficult but nevertheless essential task which would involve the specification of domains or dimensions of behaviour to be measured, the creation of tasks that sample or typify the behaviours and the relation of task performance to the behaviours. Previous efforts appear to have relied upon quite arbitrary initial specifications of the language behaviours to be measured and the 'face' validity of the test tasks. The problems of going beyond this partial and simplistic approach are formidable, as the next section will show.

READING COMPREHENSION

It has already been suggested that a problem which would unavoidably be foremost in the minds of those developing tests for monitoring at eleven and fifteen is that of the nature and structure of comprehension in reading. Those seeking to undertake or improve classroom assessment in this age range should also pay careful attention to this issue. Reading comprehension has been the subject of a long-standing controversy among researchers, which even now is far from resolved (Farr, 1969).

A disproportionately large body of tests and test-techniques already exists for the measurement of the initial and mechanical aspects of reading skill. It is true that many such tests have norms which could be applied to older readers, but they are based on skills which have been learned much earlier and which are of decreasing importance; examples are tests which require oral word- and sentence-reading.

In the more advanced stages, where the emphasis is upon silent reading and comprehension, the range and quality of assessment materials is less satisfactory. This is in part a consequence of the past tendency for the teaching of reading to be largely confined to the early stages, leaving the development of comprehension skills — a process which continues into adult reading — relatively neglected.

Rational versus empirical evidence

A current difficulty in producing credible materials at this level arises out of differences in the perspectives of those who have attempted to produce hierarchies and rationales for teaching comprehension and those who have studied it empirically by the use of tests.

The thinking of many practising teachers is probably influenced by the former viewpoint, and draws upon the intuitive analysis of reading comprehension found in classification schemes such as Barrett's (1972), rather than upon the less clear-cut maps of comprehention skills found in the research literature. Barrett defines five major levels of reading: literal comprehension, reorganization, inference, evaluation and appreciation. Further amplifications are made within each level; for example, 'reorganization' is said to involve processes of classifying, outlining, summarizing and synthesizing. There is no doubt — given the limits of our present state of knowledge — that such a drawn-up 'taxonomy' of reading processes provides an invaluable guide by which teachers can organize and structure their thinking, materials and methods in the day-to-day development of reading at this advanced, and previously most neglected, level.

To some extent such schemes are also useful in checking comprehensiveness of coverage in reading tests, or even as general guides to those who are devising test-questions. However, it is only too easy for the naïve or uniformed to assume that comprehension is really divisible into the separate psychological processes or traits postulated by the taxonomists.

Research evidence does not support this notion. Many studies have failed to identify any discrete skills or sub-skills of comprehension. More often than not, they tend to show comprehension as more of a unitary and indivisible trait. Those studies which have managed to isolate separate skills have agreed only loosely about the nature of the differences and have borne an even more tenuous relationship to any existing theoretical scheme or hierarchy. The possibility of producing 'diagnostic' or qualitative sub-scales in reading comprehension tests has thus yet to be realized, although it is undeniably a worthwhile and admirable goal.

While some of the confusion arises out of the conflicting nature of the empirical evidence, part of the difficulty must also be attributed to the necessarily arbitrary nature of any taxonomy of reading behaviour. It is indeed possible to devise, on the basis of speculation or intuition, any number of descriptions and taxonomies of reading comprehension, all of which seem sensible, but which differ according to the purposes for which they are used. It is thus not surprising that theoretical and empirical evidence are so much at odds, given the variable nature of the former.

The tension between researchers looking for the psychological realities and the reading specialists who seek to categorize for teaching purposes is one for which no easy resolution can be suggested. It is worth bearing in mind, however, that the most reasonable form of assessment will be that which seeks to measure as closely as possible what has been taught. It thus makes no sense to administer a test based on, say, Barrett's taxonomy, if a systematic programme of teaching based on this taxonomy has not first been carried out. This lack of match between curriculum and test-content may be a cause of much of the disappointment experienced by researchers into the structure of comprehension; if a pupil has not been actually taught to use each of a specified set of skills, is it not at least possible that his performance on each of the relevant sub-tests will be no more than a reflection of a general ability that manifests itself equally in all the tests?

Comprehension and intelligence

Many researchers into the structure of reading comprehension have approached the phenomenon exactly as they have studied the structure of intelligence. That is to say, they have sought to measure a range of behaviours regarded as either innate, or at least fundamental, features of the way the human intellect is organized. This may be a fair enough assumption for the study of intelligence, but, by contrast, comprehension skill may be more the outcome of systematic instruction or — more often — incidental learning. It may therefore be misguided to research or measure it as if it were no more than an analogy of human intelligence.

Processes and outcomes

Both the empiricists and the taxonomists have tended to concentrate upon the identification of different *outcomes* of reading comprehension, so that mental processes or learned behaviours can be attached or attributed to them.

A more fruitful approach to the problem might be to look for the processes themselves, and to ask in what ways a reader adopts different styles or strategies to meet the requirements of different reading tasks. In particular, it might be valuable to concentrate upon preferences for different styles and strategies exhibited by different readers following the same purpose. So far, only a little of this type of work has been done in the reading field, although the study of qualitative differences in thinking, learning and problem-solving — 'cognitive styles' — has been a major research topic in other fields of psychology. It might thus be worth devising tests to evaluate a reader's capacity to adopt the most productive strategy for the requirements of a particular reading task. As a potential source of better diagnostic information such studies of the psychology of reading strategies certainly look promising.

Some foretaste of the possibile outcomes of work in this area can be gained from research reported by Marton and Saljo (1976), which dealt with qualitative differences in the way university students tackled the reading of extended prose passages. The investigations revealed that readers tended to obtain qualitatively different information from the passages, and that their varying responses could be related to differences in the way the task was approached. The students could be divided into 'surface-level' and 'deep-level' processors. The former type tended to concentrate upon the content of the text itself, the latter upon the meanings that the content signified — upon what it was *about* rather than what it *was*. Thomas and Augstein (1972) have also studied qualitative differences in reading strategies. Their work has concentrated upon the rates and patterns of processing text: different styles of working have been shown to vary with efficiency of comprehension. They have also demonstrated that what readers extract from a text is in part influenced by their expectations of the way their understanding or retention will subsequently be tested.

The influence of the mode of testing upon comprehension is also illustrated in the work of Rothkopf (1970), who has examined some of the processes by which a reader learns from written materials ('mathemagenic' activities). This work has included studies on the way in which insertion of questions periodically throughout a text can influence, positively or negatively, what the reader understands or learns from the text.

Such research is highly experimental, and it deals with older students and adults, but it seems possible that similar phenomena would be observable among younger readers. It would be reasonable to expect, for example, that deep- or surface-level approaches to reading evolve early in a pupil's educational career.

This work may go only a little way towards elucidation of the nature of reading comprehension, but it is nevertheless thought-provoking both for teachers and test-developers. It suggests that instead of looking for a variety of different processes within the *same* reader we should consider the possibility that such differences of varieties that exist must be found in different readers — a categorizing of persons, not processes. Second, it draws attention to the need to give much more consideration to the role of questions and questioning. In experimental studies, differences in both the qualitative and quantitative outcomes of a 'read' appear to depend very much on the reader's perception of the purpose of the reading task. Thus, it seems possible that differences in the nature or extent of the questions readers spontaneously form in their minds while they read could provide a key to certain differences in comprehension ability. Diagnostic testing in future may thus have to concentrate much more upon the reader's perception of the purpose of a reading task before endeavouring to ascertain how well he carried it out.

OTHER LANGUAGE SKILLS: SPELLING

In spite of basic difficulties such as those outlined above, a much more advanced body of 'technology' is available for assessment of reading ability than is available for any other aspect of language measurement. Relatively little progress has been made in objective measurement of either written or spoken communication, and although many tests of listening skill have been produced (e.g., by the Educational Testing Service and NFER), only recently have these tests treated *listening* as the understanding of *speech* (see Wilkinson *et al.*, 1974), as distinct from a form of written prose that happens to be read aloud.

In the space of a single chapter it would not be possible to speculate at any length upon the desirable innovations in research or classroom practice that would be necessary for remedying all these defects. What are really required are schemes of assessment and observation that

(a) co-ordinate measurement in all four language channels and
(b) cover linguistic development over a wide age-range, ideally from pre-school years to the later years of secondary education.

The assessment of spelling ability would be a major element in such research and development work. Indeed, spelling standards are currently a pressing problem. Adult literacy tutors find that many students require more help with spelling than anything else, and employers and teachers in further and higher education have expressed dissatisfaction with the spelling ability of school leavers. This issue requires attention at both national and school levels, and is of sufficient priority to be singled out here as the subject for more detailed consideration.

Standardized tests

Only a few standardized tests of spelling have been produced for use in schools, and spelling standards have not, in the past, been the subject for research or monitoring on a national scale. The ideological debate concerning the importance of spelling seems to have been concluded in favour of the view that it is a 'convention that matters' (DES, 1975). It is likely, as a result, that there will be an increased demand for means of measuring spelling proficiency.

It would be unfortunate if the attempts to improve tests of spelling were to result merely in the production of up-dated versions of listening tests designed to provide spelling 'ages' or quotients, or even a national 'norm' based, say, on the number of test words a pupil was able to spell. Such results tell us too little about the state of spelling, either in a school, or nationally, to be of much use. The words employed in the test are likely to be arbitrary from an educational or linguistic standpoint whatever their statistical virtues. Further, the completion of a spelling test is a highly artificial task, which does not sample or simulate the conditions in which people are usually expected to employ spelling skills. Of the methods employed in the classroom to assess spelling, perhaps only the traditional dictation test has any claim to assess spelling in a realistic context. Even this is a limited claim. The incidence of dictation tasks, in education or daily life, is probably slight.

The validity of most extant published and standardized tests is thus open to question; there are relatively few situations in which the speller is expected to write isolated words or sentences dictated by somebody else. There are certainly some habitually poor spellers who are able to perform well under the pressures of a test situation, although once the test is over they revert to a lower level of spelling accuracy. Indeed, it has not been demonstrated empirically how closely variations in pupils' scores on standardised tests of spelling are associated with genuine differences in their standard of spelling in everyday school work. In practice, teachers and researchers have tended to take it for granted that a spelling test score is an accurate predictor of general spelling ability. One would not expect even an artificial test to be a wholly *in*accurate predictor of spelling performance in other situations, but the question of how precise or accurate such tests are has never really been answered. We do not know, for example, whether a slight difference in spelling ages, say, three or four months, is indicative of negligible, slight or drastic differences in the standard of spelling displayed in other written work. The same is true of differences measured in years.

Criterion-referenced tests

Shortcomings of existing standardized tests could, at least in part, be overcome by a more systematic approach to content. This would require carefully-devised criteria for the choice of words to be employed in the test. These might be drawn from frequency counts of words children are known to use in their writing (e.g., Edwards and Gibbon, 1968) or from published lists of words intended to form the basis of a systematic teaching scheme (e.g., Arvidson, 1960). Further alternatives would be to employ words known to be frequently mis-spelled or words that conform to rules within the English spelling system. Prototypes for many of these approaches exist, but they are far from sufficiently researched to meet the rigorous demands of what would amount to a criterion-referenced approach to testing. Each of these possiblities also has its own particular limitations. For example, words commonly used by children in their writing are unlikely to provide very discriminating test questions. Published lists are themselves essentially arbitrary criteria for spelling words; no really authoritative study of children's mis-spellings has been carried out, and problems arise in inferring that because a child spells a particular word correctly he has therefore learned the general rule that the word exemplifies. It is easy to see limitations in this approach, but it must be said that these limitations are as much a consequence of shortcomings in our knowledge of teaching spelling as of the concept on which the test is based. The least that could be done to improve matters would be to devise test methods to be more in harmony with current teaching practices, however limited these may ultimately be shown to be.

Direct sampling

Doubts have already been raised about the validity of employing a medium of testing that does not involve the speller's own spontaneous writing. It was suggested that, with the possible exception of dictation, most of the methods currently employed in tests of spelling are divorced from authentic writing tasks and that the relation they bear to the pupil's level of spelling performance in real life has yet to be proven. This naturally raises the question of how real-life spelling performance can in fact be assessed, either as a basis for validation of other tests or as a procedure to be used in its own right. A teacher's own subjective rating of pupils' proficiency might be relevant, but there is no acceptable substitute for direct appraisal of pupils' own writing if we wish to measure spelling realistically.

In principle, it would seem simple enough to measure spelling ability by carrying out a count of the frequency with which errors occur in a pupil's written work. The raw scores obtained in this way could even be related to norms and expressed in units of standard score. In practice there are a number of technical problems with such a procedure. In the first place, a work-sampling procedure would have to be sufficiently robust to be applied to schools with varied curricula, teaching methods and organization, while providing comparable results. Second, it would be necessary to evolve means of sampling that were economical in application while fairly representative of a writer's overall performance. For example, could the rate of errors displayed in three essays written at termly intervals throughout a year be taken as representative of the rate of errors displayed in all a pupil's work during the year, or are much larger and more carefully devised procedures necessary to estimate this? The goal would be to devise a short and economical sampling procedure, but this possibility would depend very much upon the consistency with which pupils were found to spell well or badly across the school curriculum; a pupil who spells impeccably in history but very poorly in biology — perhaps because of variations in motivation — would defy any simple sampling procedure. At the present time, it is not known how common such wide variations in spelling work are. It is worth reflecting that if a pupil's standard of spelling does fluctuate across tasks, the notion of spelling age based on a standardized test is all the more inappropriate. The question of sampling pupils' work to measure spelling attainment could certainly be dealt with by research, but there is no reason why some of the preliminary investigations could not be adequately carried out by teachers themselves.

Spelling processes

So far the discussion has dealt with measurement of *what* a child spells rather than how he spells — that is to say, to what extent he has the skills and qualities of a 'good' speller. Margaret Peters (1967) has been influential in drawing attention to such abilities and suggests they include the visual perception and recall of words, awareness of serial probabilities of letter occurrence and development of a concept of self as a good, rather than poor, speller. As yet there appears to have been little work into developing the means of assessing such characteristics, although for diagnostic purposes in particular, this would be very helpful. Important work might also be done through either relatively artificial tests, or by developing coding schemes for the analysis of error patterns in free writing, and again it appears to be a topic that is highly amenable to classroom-based research.

ASSESSMENT IN SCHOOL

All that has been said so far has been based on the hope that teachers may become more willing to accord a positive role to assessment. In the past, assessment has been distrusted. It was taken to be synonymous with standardized testing, with its connotations of 'eleven-plus' selection, labelling or 'writing off' of children on the strength of a single test score, and general stress and anxiety associated with being tested. One of the most telling criticisms of standardized reading tests has been that teachers are no further on once a test has been given; results may fail to convey any useful or comprehensible information, or schools may be incapable of taking any constructive action beyond the empty ritual of administration and marking of tests.

In addition, standardized testing appears to be an aspect of school practice that is resistant to change, innovation or improvement — the Bullock survey itself revealed that the most widely-used tests were also the most archaic and limited in scope. It is thus no wonder that teachers are sometimes highly dissatisfied with testing as it is carried out in their schools, and Fry (1976) makes some telling criticisms of testing that deserve some serious attention wherever testing is carried out without thought or question, or where long established practices have been regarded with complacency. Assessment should, ideally, involve very much more than standardized testing. It would be a pity if efforts at assessment were entirely abandoned just because standardized testing is prone to abuses such as those mentioned above.

In the first place, the contribution of standardized tests themselves might be made more positive if their potential role were reconsidered. The Bullock Report (DES, 1975), for example, describes how they might legitimately be employed as a screening device for the identification of pupils in need of special help.

There are other uses that merit more exploration, particularly the longitudinal use of tests with groups of pupils in order to observe progress and improvement throughout a school career, culminating in a terminal assessment. This applies particularly in the case of secondary schools, where it is perhaps too easy to regard public examination results as the sole criterion of effectiveness, thus neglecting the evaluation of standards among younger pupils or those who eventually take few examination subjects. This notion of a terminal or 'summative', assessment of reading standards is widely established in primary schools and deserves more serious attention at secondary level. A school might learn much in the long run about the effectiveness of its contributions to the literacy of its pupils in this way. It would thus be possible to introduce the enlightened uses of standardized testing and, indeed, more judicious application of existing practices. For this to happen, it would be necessary for teachers to receive very much more efficient training in testing than is anywhere available at present. It would be desirable for proficiency in standardized testing to become, in the long run, as much a part of the reading specialist's professional skill as other, more obvious, attributes. Unfortunately, until this happens, standardized testing will tend to be more a liability in schools than an asset.

Beyond standardized testing

So far the discussion has dealt with improvements in the use of standardized testing. The most important way in which reading assessment would be improved, however, is by treating standardized testing as only a single component in a larger programme or policy of assessment which included a range of diagnostic and evaluative techniques. The Bullock Report itself draws attention to some of these, particularly the analysis of reading 'miscues' and the informal reading inventory (or IRI). The IRI, for example, enables the teacher to estimate directly the degree to which a reader can deal effectively with any particular text, and it is the *procedure* for doing this, rather than the material itself, that is standardized. In essence, it requires the child to read the chosen passage(s) aloud and answer a series of systematically devised questions. The guidelines for interpretation allow the teacher to estimate the suitability of the text for any given purpose; for example, oral reading with 95 to 98 per cent accuracy might indicate that a passage was suitable for 'instructional' use — that is, as material for practising and extending reading skills. A useful account of many of the possible elaborations and extensions of the technique has been provided by Pumfrey (1976). One of the most promising developments of the IRI approach is in the technique for analysis of reading errors or 'miscues' developed by Goodman and Burke (1970). This involves the interpretation of reading performance in terms of the system of cues the reader employs, rather than in simplistic phonic terms. A similar approach is exemplified in work by Clay (1972a, b), which concentrates upon close observation of individual reading strategies, notably the use of self-correction. Also, in recent years reading teachers and researchers have shown considerable interest in cloze procedure, in which words are deleted from a prose passage and the reader endeavours to guess the missing words. Like the IRI, cloze can be a general method to be used on the particular materials with which the teacher is concerned rather than a standardized set-piece type of test. As with the IRI, a large number of variations on the basic technique are possible, and there is still much that remains to be learned about its diagnostic possibilities. The structured, but clinical and diagnostic, approach which such techniques exemplify clearly could have a much greater part to play in reading assessment, with proportionally less emphasis placed upon normative and statistical measurement.

This is a much stonier path to tread, for both the test-developer and the teacher. The development and application of a standardized test can become a routine operation, once the basic psychometric principles have been grasped. Creating new diagnostic techniques and materials would require fundamental and imaginative research involved much more deeply in the actual psychology and pedagogy of reading. The materials or techniques that emerge from such enterprises are likely to be much more demanding upon the teacher, as well as more useful. The informal inventory, for example, requires much more initiative and effort on the part of teachers than, say, a standardized test. Similarly, the analysis of reading miscues (Goodman and Burke, 1970) requires practice, skill and commitment if it is to be of any use.

Improvement in reading assessment will thus demand much more of teachers, and the accent would be upon a do-it-yourself technology (item-banking, cloze and informal reading inventories provide diverse examples of this) rather than upon published tests in their traditional finished form. The long-term success of this approach will depend very largely upon the extent to which it can be fostered and supported through workshops, study groups and training courses. It would not be enough to publish a set of materials or a guide to a new technique and hope for the best. Unless these further steps are taken to develop skill, confidence and commitment, their real impact will be slight.

It is a commonplace observation that educational innovations succeed most readily when practised by teachers who are committed to them. The same is true of assessment in the teaching of reading. Standardized testing failed to earn acceptance as widely as it might have done partly because it arrived in school unheralded by discussion and unaccompanied by explanation. It is true that standardized testing is not always the approach that teachers want, but such virtues that it does have are easily underestimated because there has not been enough effort to interest and involve teachers in their exploitation. It would be a pity if more enlightened or promising approaches to assessment were to meet the same fate. This could be avoided if assessment became something that teachers were trained to do, rather than just made to do.

References

Arvidson, G. L. (1960) *Learning to Spell* (NZCER Studies in Education, 12). New Zealand: NZCER.
Barrett, T. C. (1972) In Clymer, T. 'What is "reading?"' Some current concepts,' *Reading Today and Tomorrow* Melnik, L. A. and Merritt, J., Eds. London: University of London Press.
Bormuth, J. R. (1969) 'An operational definition of comprehensive instruction,' In *Psycholinguistics and the Teaching of Reading* Goodman, K. S. and Fleming, J. F., Eds. Newark, Delaware: International Reading Association.
Bormuth, J. R. (1973) 'Reading literacy: its definition and assessment, *Reading Research Quarterly*, 9, 7–66.
Clay, M. M. (1972a) *Reading: The Patterning of Complex Behaviour*. Auckland: Heinemann.
Clay, M. M. (1972b) *A Diagnostic Survey*. Auckland: Heinemann.
Des (1975) *A Language for Life* (The Bullock Report). London: HMSO.
Edwards, R. P. A. and Gibbon, V. (1968) *Words Your Children Use*. London: Burke.
English Proficiency Tests, Listening. Slough: NFER.
Farr, R. (1969) *Reading: What Can be Measured?* Newark, Delaware: International Reading Association.
Fry, D. (1976) 'Against the testing of reading,' *The Urban Review*, 9, 2.
Goodman, Y. and Burke, C. (1970) *Reading Miscues Inventory*. New York: Macmillan.
Lunzer, E. A. and Gardner, K., Eds. (1977) *The Effective Use of Reading* (Draft Report to Schools Council). University of Nottingham School of Education.

MacFarlane, T. (1976) 'Reading skills: automatic transfer up a hierarchy?" *Reading*, 10, No. 3, 12–19.

Marton, F. and Saljo, R. (1976) 'On qualitative differences in learning: I — outcome and process,' *British Journal of Educational Psychology, 46*, 4–11.

Nicholls, A. (1975) 'A survey of reading tests used in schools.' In *Reading: What of the Future?* Moyle, D., Ed. London: Ward Lock Educational.

Peters, M. L. (1967) *Spelling: Caught, or Taught?* London: Routledge.

Pumfrey, P. D. (1976) *Reading Tests and Assessment Techniques*. London: Hodder and Stoughton.

Rothkopf, E. Z. (1970) 'The concept of mathemagenic activities,' *Review of Educational Research, 4*, 325–36.

Schofield, R. S. (1968), 'The measurement of literacy in pre-industrial England.' In *Literacy in Traditional Societies*. Goody, J., Ed. London: Cambridge University Press.

Sequential Tests of Educational Progress: Listening. Princeton, New Jersey: Educational Testing Service.

Start, K. B. and Wells, B. K. (1972) *The Trend of Reading Standards* 1970–71. Slough: NFER.

Thomas, L. and Augstein, S. (1972) 'An experimental approach to the study of reading as a learning skill,' *Research in Education, 8*, 28–46.

Wilkinson, A., Stratta, L. and Dudley, P. (1974) *The Quality of Listening*. London: Macmillan.

Further
Reading

The reference lists at the end of each chapter supply a number of leads for students and other interested readers who wish to pursue topics discussed in them. However, for those who seek advice on the best route into further reading, the following list of books, selected chapter by chapter, offers the likeliest (and usually the most accessible) way of starting.

Chapter 1

Blank, M. (1973) *Teaching Learning in the Preschool: A Dialogue Approach*. Columbus, Ohio: Charles Merrill.
Keddie, N., Ed. (1973) *Tinker, Tailor . . .* Harmondsworth: Penguin Books.
Pidgeon, D. A. (1970) *Expectation and Pupil Performance*. Slough: NFER.

Chapter 2

Crystal, D. (1976) *Child Language, Learning and Linguistics*. London: Edward Arnold.
Trudgill, P. (1975) *Accent, Dialect and the School*. London: Edward Arnold.

Chapter 3

Gibson, E. J. and Levin, H. (1975) *The Psychology of Reading*. Cambridge, Mass: MIT Press.

Smith, F. (1978) *Understanding Reading* (2nd Edition). New York: Holt, Rinehart and Winston.

Kavanagh, J. F. and Mattingley, I. G. (1972) *Language by Ear and by Eye*. Cambridge, Mass: MIT Press.

Chapter 4

Rosen, C. and H. (1973) *The Language of Primary School Children*. Harmondsworth: Penguin Books.

Jones, A. and Mulford, J., Eds. (1971) *Children Using Language: An Approach to English in the Primary School*. London: Oxford University Press.

Jones, A. and Buttrey, J. (1970) *Children and Stories*. London: Basil Blackwell.

Chapter 5

Longley, C., Ed. (1977) *Reading after Ten*. London: BBC Publications.

Lunzer, E. A. and Gardner, W. K., Eds. (1978) *The Effective Use of Reading*. London: Heinemann Educational.

Marland, M. (1977) *Language Across the Curriculum*. London: Heinemann Educational.

Chapter 6

Hourd, M. (1972) *Relationship in Learning*. London: Heinemann.

Hughes, T. (1967) *Poetry in the Making*. London: Faber.

Witkin, R. (1974) *The Intelligence of Feeling*. London: Heinemann.

Chapter 7

Barnes, D., Britton, J. N. and Rosen, H. (1971) *Language, the Learner and the School*. Harmondsworth: Penguin Books.

Martin, N. C. *et al* (1976) *Writing and Learning Across the Curriculum*. London: Ward Lock Educational.

Chapter 8

Gibson, E. J. and Levin, H. (1975) *The Psychology of Reading*. Cambridge, Mass: MIT Press.
Halliday, M. A. K. and Hasan, R. (1976) *Cohesion in English*. London: Longman.
Widdowson, H. G. (1978) *Teaching Language as Communication*. London: OUP.

Chapter 9

Pumfrey, P. D. (1977) *Measuring Reading Abilities: Concepts, Sources and Applications*. London: Hodder and Stoughton Educational.
Farr, R. (1969) *Reading: What can be Measured?* Newark: International Reading Association.
Raggett, M., Tutt, C., and Raggett, P. A., Eds. (1979) *Testing Reading – Problems and Practices*. London: Ward Lock Educational.

Contributors

Asher Cashdan is Head of the Department of Communication Studies, Sheffield City Polytechnic.

David Crystal is Professor of Linguistic Science at the University of Reading.

Geoffrey Roberts is a Senior Lecturer in Education at the University of Manchester.

Elizabeth Grugeon is an Educational Consultant working at the Open University.

David Grugeon is Deputy Director of Studies, Regional Tutorial Services, The Open University.

Eric Lunzer is Professor of Educational Psychology at the University of Nottingham.

Terry Dolan is a Lecturer in Education at the University of Nottingham.

Bernard Harrison is a Lecturer in English in Education at the University of Sheffield.

Mike Torbe is Curriculum Development Officer for Coventry.

Alan Davies is a Senior Lecturer in Linguistics at Edinburgh University.

Denis Vincent is a Senior Research Officer at the National Foundation for Educational Research in England and Wales.

161

Index

Abercrombie, D., 122, 134

Accent, classroom, 6

Adult language, 3, 17–18, 77–8

'Advanced organizers' method, 42, 63

Allen, J. P. B., 124, 134

Anti-grammar movement, the, 125

Applebee, R., 81, 86

Armstrong, M., 106, 118

'Arts and the Adolescent', project on, 91

Arvidson, G. L., 150, 156

Assessment, 76, 132, 137–56; age-related, 141–2, 144, 149; comprehension, 137, 144–8; 'criterion-referenced', 132, 139–44, 150–1; IRI, 154–5; literacy, 142–5; national monitoring of, 137–56; question banks for, 139–40; spelling, 138, 148–52; standards of, 137–56

Augstein, S., 67, 74, 75, 87, 147–8, 157

Ausubel, D. P., 42, 45

Barnes, D., 105, 116, 118

Barrett, T. C., 145–6, 156

Bartlett, F. C., 34, 45

Bennett, N., 9, 11

Berg, L., 122, 134